CAMBRIDGE
UNIVERSITY PRESS

CAMBRIDGE ENGLISH
Language Assessment
Part of the University of Cambridge

Cambridge English

KEY ENGLISH TEST

WITH ANSWERS

AUTHEN... ...APERS
FROM ... ...SH
LA... ...T

Cambridge University Press
www.cambridge.org/elt

Cambridge English Language Assessment
www.cambridgeenglish.org

Information on this title: www.cambridge.org/9781107664944

© Cambridge University Press and UCLES 2014

It is normally necessary for written permission for copying to be obtained
in advance from a publisher. The sample answer sheets at the back of this
book are designed to be copied and distributed in class.
The normal requirements are waived here and it is not necessary to write to
Cambridge University Press for permission for an individual teacher to make copies
for use within his or her own classroom. Only those pages that carry the wording
'© UCLES 2014 Photocopiable' may be copied.

First published 2014
Reprinted 2016

Printed in Italy by Rotolito Lombarda S.p.A.

A catalogue record for this publication is available from the British Library

ISBN 978-1-107-66494-4 Student's Book with answers
ISBN 978-1-107-64185-3 Student's Book without answers
ISBN 978-1-107-64176-1 Audio CD
ISBN 978-1-107-69198-8 Student's Book Pack (Student's Book with answers and Audio CD)

The publishers have no responsibility for the persistence or accuracy
of URLs for external or third-party internet websites referred to in this publication,
and do not guarantee that any content on such websites is, or will remain,
accurate or appropriate. Information regarding prices, travel timetables, and other
factual information given in this work is correct at the time of first printing but
the publishers do not guarantee the accuracy of such information thereafter.

Contents

Key 7 Acknowledgements

The authors and publishers acknowledge the following sources of copyright material and are grateful for the permissions granted. While every effort has been made, it has not always been possible to identify the sources of all the material used, or to trace all copyright holders. If any omissions are brought to our notice, we will be happy to include the appropriate acknowledgements on reprinting.

The publishers are grateful to the following for permission to reproduce copyright photographs and material:

p. 17: Alamy/© Mint Photography; p. 20: Alamy/© Christopher Perks; p. 37: SuperStock/© SuperStock; p. 42: Shutterstock/© moizhusein; p. 57: SuperStock/© Kablonk; p. 60: Newscom/© ERDEN ERUC/UPI; p. 62: Shutterstock/© Rudi Venter; p. 77: Corbis/© Blaine Harrington III; p. 82: SuperStock/© Wolfgang Kaehler.

Book design by Peter Ducker MSTD

Cover design by David Lawton

The CD which accompanies this book was recorded at dsound, London.

A guide to Cambridge English: Key

Cambridge English: Key, also known as the *Key English Test (KET)*, is part of a comprehensive range of exams developed by Cambridge English Language Assessment. Cambridge English exams have similar characteristics but are designed for different purposes and different levels of English language ability. *Cambridge English: Key* is at Level A2 (Waystage) of the Council of Europe's Common European Framework of Reference for Languages (CEFR). It has also been accredited in the UK as an Entry Level 2 ESOL certificate in the UK's National Qualifications Framework.

Examination	Council of Europe Framework Level	UK National Qualifications Framework Level
Cambridge English: Proficiency *Certificate of Proficiency in English (CPE)*	C2	3
Cambridge English: Advanced *Certificate in Advanced English (CAE)*	C1	2
Cambridge English: First *First Certificate in English (FCE)*	B2	1
Cambridge English: Preliminary *Preliminary English Test (PET)*	B1	Entry 3
Cambridge English: Key *Key English Test (KET)*	A2	Entry 2

Cambridge English: Key is accepted by employers, further education and government departments for business, study and immigration purposes. It is also useful preparation for higher level exams, such as *Cambridge English: Preliminary* and *Cambridge English: First*.

Cambridge English: Key is a great first step in English. Preparing for the exam will build your confidence in dealing with everyday written and spoken English at a basic level, for example expressing and understanding simple opinions; filling in forms; and writing short, simple letters.

Cambridge English: Key is also available in a version with exam content and topics specifically targeted at the interests and experience of school-aged learners. *Cambridge English: Key for Schools*, also known as the *Key English Test (KET) for Schools*, follows exactly the same format and level and leads to the same certificate as *Cambridge English: Key*.

Topics

These are the topics used in the *Cambridge English: Key* exam:

Clothes	People	Shopping
Daily life	Personal feelings, opinions	Social interaction
Entertainment and media	and experiences	The natural world
Food and drink	Personal identification	Transport
Health, medicine and exercise	Places and buildings	Travel and holidays
Hobbies and leisure	School and study	Weather
House and home	Services	Work and jobs
Language		

Overview of the exam

Paper	Name	Timing	Content	Test focus
Paper 1	Reading / Writing	1 hour 10 minutes	Nine parts: Five parts (Parts 1–5) test a range of reading skills with a variety of texts, ranging from very short notices to longer continuous texts. Parts 6–9 concentrate on testing basic writing skills.	Assessment of candidates' ability to understand the meaning of written English at word, phrase, sentence, paragraph and whole text level. Assessment of candidates' ability to produce simple written English, ranging from one-word answers to a short piece of continuous text.
Paper 2	Listening	30 minutes (including 8 minutes transfer time)	Five parts, ranging from short exchanges to longer dialogues and monologues.	Assessment of candidates' ability to understand dialogues and monologues in both informal and neutral settings on a range of everyday topics.
Paper 3	Speaking	8–10 minutes per pair of candidates	Two parts: In Part 1, candidates interact with an examiner. In Part 2, they interact with another candidate.	Assessment of candidates' ability to answer and ask questions about themselves and about factual, non-personal information.

Paper 1 Reading and Writing

Paper format

The Reading section contains five parts. The Writing section contains four parts.

Number of questions

There is a total of 56 questions: 35 in Reading and 21 in Writing.

Sources

Authentic and adapted-authentic real-world notices, newspaper and magazine articles, simplified encyclopaedia entries.

Answering

Candidates indicate answers either by shading lozenges (Reading) or by writing answers (Writing) on an answer sheet.

Timing

1 hour 10 minutes.

Marks

Each item carries one mark, except for question 56 (Part 9), which is marked out of 5. This gives a total of 60 marks, which is weighted to a final mark out of 50. This represents 50% of the total marks for the whole examination.

Preparing for the Reading section

To prepare for the Reading section, you should read the type of English used in everyday life; for example, short newspaper and magazine articles, advertisements, tourist brochures, instructions and recipes, etc. It is also a good idea to practise reading short communicative messages, including notes, emails and cards. Remember, you won't always need to understand every word to be able to do a task in the exam.

Before the exam, think about the time you need to do each part and check you know how to record your answers on the answer sheet (see page 148).

Part	Task type and format	Task focus	Number of questions
1	Matching. Matching five prompt sentences to eight notices, plus an example.	Gist understanding of real-world notices. Reading for main message.	5
2	Three-option multiple choice. Five sentences (plus an integrated example) with connecting link of topic or storyline.	Reading and identifying appropriate vocabulary.	5

3	Three-option multiple choice. Five discrete three-option multiple-choice items (plus an example) focusing on verbal exchange patterns. **AND** Matching. Five matching items (plus an example) in a continuous dialogue, selecting from eight possible responses.	Functional language. Reading and identifying the appropriate response.	10
4	Right / Wrong / Doesn't say **OR** Three-option multiple choice. One long text or three short texts adapted from authentic newspaper or magazine articles. Seven three-option multiple-choice items or Right / Wrong / Doesn't say items, plus an example.	Reading for detailed understanding and main idea(s).	7
5	Multiple-choice cloze. A text adapted from an original source, for example an encyclopaedia entry, newspaper or magazine article. Eight three-option multiple-choice items, plus an integrated example.	Reading and identifying appropriate structural words (auxiliary verbs, modal verbs, determiners, pronouns, prepositions, conjunctions, etc.).	8

Preparing for the Writing section

To prepare for the Writing section, you should take the opportunity to write short messages in real-life situations, for example to your teacher or other students. These can include invitations, arrangements for meetings, apologies for missing a class, or notices about lost property. They can be handwritten or sent as email.

Before the exam, think about the time you need to do each part and check you know how to record your answers on the answer sheet (see page 149).

Part	Task type and format	Task focus	Number of questions
6	Word completion. Five dictionary definition type sentences (plus an example). Five words to identify and spell.	Reading and identifying appropriate vocabulary, and spelling.	5
7	Open cloze. Text type that candidates can be expected to write, for example a short letter or email. Ten spaces to fill with one word which must be spelled correctly, (plus an integrated example).	Reading and identifying appropriate words, with a focus on structure and / or vocabulary.	10
8	Information transfer. Two short authentic texts (emails, adverts, etc.) to prompt completion of another text (form, note, etc.). Five spaces to fill with one or more words or numbers (plus an integrated example).	Reading and writing appropriate words or numbers, with a focus on content and accuracy.	5
9	Guided writing. Either a short input text or a rubric to prompt a written response. Three messages to communicate in writing.	Writing a short message, note, email or postcard of 25–35 words.	1

Part 6

This part is about vocabulary. You have to produce words and spell them correctly. The words will all be linked to the same topic, for example jobs or food. You have to read a definition for each one and complete the word. The first letter of each word is given to help you.

Part 7

This part is about grammar and vocabulary. You have to complete a short, gapped text of the type you could be expected to write, such as a note, email or short letter. You must spell all the missing words correctly.

A guide to Cambridge English: Key

Part 8

This part tests both reading and writing. You have to use the information in two short texts (for example a note, email or advertisement) to complete a document such as a form, notice or diary entry. You will need to understand the vocabulary used on forms, for example *name*, *cost* and *time*. You will need to write only words or phrases in your answers, but you must spell them correctly.

Part 9

You have to write a short message (25–35 words). You are told who you are writing to and why, and you must include three pieces of information. To gain top marks, all three parts of the message must be included in your answer, so it is important to read the question carefully and plan what you are going to write. Before the exam, practise writing answers of the correct length. You will lose marks for writing fewer than 25 words, and it is not a good idea to write answers that are too long.

Mark Scheme for Part 9

There are five marks for Part 9. Minor grammatical and spelling mistakes are acceptable, but to get five marks you must write a clear message and include all three pieces of information.

Mark	Criteria	
5	All three parts of the message clearly communicated. Only minor spelling errors or occasional grammatical errors.	
4	All three parts of the message communicated. Some non-impeding errors in spelling and grammar or some awkwardness of expression.	
3	All three parts of the message attempted. Expression requires interpretation by the reader and contains impeding errors in spelling and grammar.	Two parts of the message clearly communicated. Only minor spelling errors or occasional grammatical errors.
2	Only two parts of the message communicated. Some errors in spelling and grammar. The errors in expression may require patience and interpretation by the reader and impede communication.	
1	Only one part of the message communicated.	
0	Question unattempted, or totally incomprehensible response.	

Paper 2   Listening

Paper format
This paper contains five parts.

Number of questions
25

Task types
Matching, multiple choice, gap-fill.

Sources
All texts are based on authentic situations, and each part is heard twice.

Answering
Candidates indicate answers either by shading lozenges (Parts 1–3) or by writing answers (Parts 4 and 5) on an answer sheet.

Timing
About 30 minutes, including 8 minutes to transfer answers.

Marks
Each item carries one mark. This gives a total of 25 marks, which represents 25% of the total marks for the examination.

Preparing for the Listening test

The best preparation for the Listening test is to listen to authentic spoken English for your level. Apart from in class, other sources of English include films, TV, DVDs, songs, the internet, English clubs, and other speakers of English such as tourists, guides, friends and family.

You will hear the instructions for each task on the recording and see them on the exam paper. There are pauses in the recording to give you time to look at the questions and to write your answers. You should write your answers on the exam paper as you listen. You will have eight minutes at the end of the test to transfer your answers to the answer sheet (see page 150). Make sure you know how to do this and that you check your answers carefully.

Part	Task type and format	Task focus	Number of questions
1	Three-option multiple choice. Short, neutral or informal dialogues. Five discrete three-option multiple-choice items with pictures (plus an example).	Listening to identify key information (times, prices, days of week, numbers, etc.).	5
2	Matching. Longer informal dialogue. Five items (plus an integrated example) and eight options.	Listening to identify key information.	5
3	Three-option multiple choice. Longer informal or neutral dialogue. Five three-option multiple-choice items (plus an integrated example).	Taking the role of one of the speakers and listening to identify key information.	5
4	Gap-fill. Longer neutral or informal dialogue. Five gaps to fill with one or more words or numbers (plus an integrated example). Recognisable spelling is accepted, except with very high-frequency words (e.g. *bus*, *red*) or if spelling is dictated.	Listening and writing down information (including spelling of names, places, etc. as dictated on recording).	5
5	Gap-fill. Longer neutral or informal monologue. Five gaps to fill with one or more words or numbers (plus an integrated example). Recognisable spelling is accepted, except with very high-frequency words (e.g. *bus*, *red*) or if spelling is dictated.	Listening and writing down information (including spelling of names, places, etc. as dictated on recording).	5

Paper 3   Speaking

Paper format

The paper contains two parts. The standard format for Paper 3 is two candidates and two examiners. One examiner acts only as an assessor and does not join in the conversation. The other examiner is called the interlocutor and manages the interaction by asking questions and setting up the tasks (see Paper 3 frames on pages 104–115).

Task types

Short exchanges with the interlocutor and an interactive task involving both candidates.

Timing

8–10 minutes per pair of candidates.

Marks

Candidates are assessed on their performance throughout the test. There are a total of 25 marks, making 25% of the total score for the whole examination.

Preparing for the Speaking test

Take every opportunity to practise your English with as many people as possible. Asking and answering questions in simple role plays provides useful practice. These role plays should focus on everyday language and situations, and involve questions about daily activities and familiar experiences. It is also a good idea to practise exchanging information in role plays about things such as the costs and opening times of, for example, a local sports centre.

Part	Task type and format	Task focus	Timing
1	Each candidate interacts with the interlocutor. The interlocutor asks the candidates questions. The interlocutor follows an interlocutor frame to guide the conversation, ensure standardisation, and control the level of input.	Language normally associated with meeting people for the first time, giving information of a factual, personal kind. Bio-data type questions to respond to.	5–6 minutes
2	Candidates interact with each other. The interlocutor sets up the activity using a standardised rubric. Candidates ask and answer questions using prompt material.	Factual information of a non-personal kind related to daily life.	3–4 minutes

Assessment

Throughout the Speaking test the examiners listen to what you say and give you marks for how well you speak English, so you must try to speak about the tasks and answer the examiner's and your partner's questions.

The two examiners mark different aspects of your speaking. One of the examiners (the assessor) will give marks on the following:

Grammar and Vocabulary

This refers to the range of language you use and also how accurately you use grammar and vocabulary.

Pronunciation

This refers to how easy it is to understand what you say. You should be able to say words and sentences that are easy to understand.

Interactive Communication

This refers to how well you can talk about a task, and to your partner and the examiner, and whether you can ask for repetition or clarification if needed.

Band	Grammar and Vocabulary	Pronunciation	Interactive Communication
5	• Shows a good degree of control of simple grammatical forms. • Uses a range of appropriate vocabulary when talking about everyday situations.	• Is mostly intelligible, and has some control of phonological features at both utterance and word levels.	• Maintains simple exchanges. • Requires very little prompting and support.
4	*Performance shares features of Bands 3 and 5.*		
3	• Shows sufficient control of simple grammatical forms. • Uses appropriate vocabulary to talk about everyday situations.	• Is mostly intelligible, despite limited control of phonological features.	• Maintains simple exchanges, despite some difficulty. • Requires prompting and support.
2	*Performance shares features of Bands 1 and 3.*		
1	• Shows only limited control of a few grammatical forms. • Uses a vocabulary of isolated words and phrases.	• Has very limited control of phonological features and is often unintelligible.	• Has considerable difficulty maintaining simple exchanges. • Requires additional prompting and support.
0	*Performance below Band 1.*		

The examiner asking the questions (the interlocutor) gives marks for how well you do overall, using a Global Achievement scale.

Band	Global Achievement
5	• Handles communication in everyday situations, despite hesitation. • Constructs longer utterances but is not able to use complex language except in well-rehearsed utterances.
4	*Performance shares features of Bands 3 and 5.*
3	• Conveys basic meaning in very familiar everyday situations. • Produces utterances which tend to be very short – words or phrases – with frequent hesitation and pauses.
2	*Performance shares features of Bands 1 and 3.*
1	• Has difficulty conveying basic meaning even in very familiar everyday situations. • Responses are limited to short phrases or isolated words with frequent hesitation and pauses.
0	*Performance below Band 1.*

Further information

The information in this practice book is designed to give an overview of *Cambridge English: Key*. For a full description of all the *Cambridge English* exams, including information about task types, testing focus and preparation, please see the relevant handbooks which can be obtained from Cambridge English Language Assessment at the address below or from the website: www.cambridgeenglish.org.

Cambridge English
Language Assessment
1 Hills Road
Cambridge
CB1 2EU
United Kingdom

Telephone: +44 1223 553355
Fax: +44 1223 460278
Email: helpdesk@cambridgeenglish.org

Test 1

PAPER 1   READING AND WRITING (1 hour 10 minutes)

PART 1

QUESTIONS 1–5

Which notice (A–H) says this (1–5)?
For questions 1–5, mark the correct letter A–H on your answer sheet.

Example:

0   You can't see this in the morning.

Answer: **0**   A B C D E F G H
☐☐☐☐■☐☐☐

---

1   Teenagers can go in here alone.

A
> Star Cinema
> New staff member wanted
> to work evenings

B
> **This way to staff car park**
> **No exit for cinema customers**

2   Get your tickets here if you've already paid to see the film.

C
> Booked online by credit card?
> Collect tickets from machine
> near entrance

3   This place doesn't open in the mornings.

D
> **Special Offer!**
> Teenagers – ask staff about discounts
> on tickets

E
> Children's film
> No tickets left for 11 a.m. show
> – afternoon show only

4   You can only use this door if you work here.

F
> **Cash only**
> **when paying for sweets**

5   You can't use a credit card here.

G
> Snack bar
> Food available from 3 p.m. weekends
> and 5 p.m. weekdays

H
> Children under 12 may only
> see this film with an adult.

PART 2

QUESTIONS 6–10

Read the sentences about travelling by plane.
Choose the best word (A, B or C) for each space.
For questions 6–10, mark A, B or C on your answer sheet.

Example:

0 Richard often travels to Canada to .... his family.

   A   stay   **B**   visit   **C**   spend   *Answer:*   **0**

	A	B	C
0	☐	■	☐

---

6 The airport gets very .... at weekends, so Richard travels during the week when it's quieter.

   A   busy   **B**   strong   **C**   heavy

7 Richard .... has a coffee when he arrives at the airport.

   A   already   **B**   once   **C**   usually

8 Richard .... looking around the shops before he gets on the plane.

   A   hopes   **B**   enjoys   **C**   wants

9 Richard hates it when there's a ...., as he likes to arrive on time.

   A   difference   **B**   moment   **C**   delay

10 Richard often watches films during the flight, or .... to the person next to him.

   A   says   **B**   tells   **C**   talks

PART 3

QUESTIONS 11–15

Complete the five conversations.
For questions 11–15, mark A, B or C on your answer sheet.

Example:

0

Where do you come from?

A New York.

B School.

C Home.

Answer:

---

11 We've just missed the 3 p.m. train.

    A Shall I get it?

    B In about an hour.

    C Then let's get the next one.

12 Do you want to come to the shops with us?

    A That would be great.

    B I don't mind it.

    C Not very often.

13 I haven't finished packing my suitcase yet.

    A I'll take you on holiday.

    B When did it happen?

    C Well, hurry up then.

14 My sister's just had a baby!

    A How lovely!

    B I'd love to!

    C Yes, she does!

15 Is that Shelley in the blue coat?

    A This is Amanda speaking.

    B She doesn't want to.

    C I think it may be.

QUESTIONS 16–20

Complete the conversation.
What does Ben say to his mother?
For questions 16–20, mark the correct letter A–H on your answer sheet.

Example:

Mother: So, Ben, did you enjoy your first day back at school?

Ben: 0 ....**D**.............

Answer:

	A B C D E F G H
0	☐☐☐■☐☐☐☐

Mother: Oh, that's good. Are there any new students?

Ben: **16** ....

Mother: Really? Do you think you'll be friends?

Ben: **17** ....

Mother: Why don't you invite him to go at the weekend instead?

Ben: **18** ....

Mother: I'm sure I can find time for that.

Ben: **19** ....

Mother: Good idea. Now, have you got any homework?

Ben: **20** ....

Mother: I'd prefer you to do your homework now, please.

A   Maybe. I'm going to ask if he wants to go swimming with me tomorrow.

B   Yes, it's too easy for me.

C   Alright. Will you be able to drive us?

D   Yes, it was fine. We've got some great new teachers.

E   Just a little. Can I watch TV first?

F   Where shall I meet him?

G   Just one. We sat next to each other.

H   I'll see what he thinks tomorrow then.

PART 4

QUESTIONS 21–27

Read the article about a young racing driver.
Are sentences 21–27 'Right' (A) or 'Wrong' (B)?
If there is not enough information to answer 'Right' (A) or 'Wrong' (B), choose
'Doesn't say' (C).
For questions 21–27, mark A, B or C on your answer sheet.

Jann Mardenborough

Jann Mardenborough has loved cars since he was given a toy one as a baby. He loved them so much that when he was eight his father took him to a place where children race small cars called karts. Staff at the kart centre told Jann he drove so well, he might one day become a racing driver. Unfortunately, the kart centre closed soon afterwards, and there wasn't another one near enough to his home that he could get to.

As he couldn't race karts any more, Jann decided to try computer racing games. After lots of practice, he became very good. However, he never told his parents what he was doing. Then, one day, when he was 18, he told them that he was one of the top ten winners of a computer racing competition. They were very surprised. His prize was to drive a real car in a race against the other nine top players.

It was Jann's first time in a racing car, but, amazingly, he won the race! The prize this time was a free course to learn to be a racing driver. He did really well, and has found a job driving in a racing team.

Example:

0   Jann's love of cars started with a toy.

    A   Right   **B**   Wrong   **C**   Doesn't say   *Answer:* **0**

	A	B	C
0	■	☐	☐

---

21   When he was a child, workers at the kart centre said Jann was a good driver.

    A   Right   **B**   Wrong   **C**   Doesn't say

22   Jann stopped racing karts because he became bored with it.

    A   Right   **B**   Wrong   **C**   Doesn't say

23   Jann was good at computer racing games immediately.

    A   Right   **B**   Wrong   **C**   Doesn't say

24   Jann played computer racing games with school friends.

    A   Right   **B**   Wrong   **C**   Doesn't say

25   Jann told his parents about the computer competition after it ended.

    A   Right   **B**   Wrong   **C**   Doesn't say

26   The people Jann raced against were from different countries.

    A   Right   **B**   Wrong   **C**   Doesn't say

27   Jann's parents had to pay for his driving course.

    A   Right   **B**   Wrong   **C**   Doesn't say

PART 5

QUESTIONS 28–35

Read the article about the history of chocolate.
Choose the best word (A, B or C) for each space.
For questions 28–35, mark A, B or C on your answer sheet.

The History
of Chocolate

The history of chocolate began **(0)** .... three and a half thousand years ago. At that time, people in the Americas **(28)** .... as the Mayans and the Aztecs grew the beans and made chocolate drinks **(29)** .... them. Around 1500, Christopher Columbus took cocoa beans to Europe, and chocolate drinks **(30)** .... became popular in Spain. However, it wasn't until nearly 100 years **(31)** .... that people started drinking chocolate in **(32)** .... parts of Europe.

In 1657, a Frenchman opened the first chocolate house in London. The drink was expensive, so only rich people **(33)** .... enjoy it. Chocolate continued to become more popular, **(34)** .... it wasn't until 1847 that the first modern chocolate bar was **(35)** .... Now chocolate is available everywhere, and we also eat it in foods like cakes, biscuits and sweets.

Example:

| 0 | **A** above | **B** between | **C** over | *Answer:* |

0 [ ][ ][■] A B C

---

28 **A** such **B** most **C** much

29 **A** by **B** in **C** from

30 **A** soon **B** ever **C** already

31 **A** late **B** later **C** latest

32 **A** both **B** other **C** every

33 **A** must **B** need **C** could

34 **A** but **B** because **C** when

35 **A** making **B** make **C** made

PART 6

QUESTIONS 36–40

Read the descriptions of some words about spending time outdoors.
What is the word for each one?
The first letter is already there. There is one space for each other letter in the word.
For questions 36–40, write the words on your answer sheet.

Example:

0   You can do this activity in the sea or in a pool.   s __ __ __ __ __ __ __

Answer: | **0** | s w i m m i n g |

---

36   This is by the sea and you can lie here in the sun.   b __ __ __ __

37   You sleep in a tent when you do this activity.   c __ __ __ __ __ __

38   You take this meal with you and eat it outside.   p __ __ __ __ __

39   This place has grass and trees and people go there to enjoy   p __ __ __
being outside.

40   You play this sport with a racket and ball.   t __ __ __ __ __

PART 7

QUESTIONS 41–50

Complete the letter.
Write ONE word for each space.
For questions 41–50, write the words on your answer sheet.

Example: | **0** | m e |

Dear Aunt Fabienne,

Mum asked **(0)** .... to let you know that I arrived home okay.

I enjoyed travelling back **(41)** .... train, and I was surprised that

(42) .... only took me three hours to get home. Thank you very

(43) .... for looking after me **(44)** .... I was in France.

I'm going back to school **(45)** .... week. My French is a lot better

(46) .... it was before, so I hope my marks will improve!

I **(47)** .... like to keep practising French and I'm looking **(48)** .... a

pen friend. I thought of your friend's son Elian. We can send emails once a

week. Let me know **(49)** .... you think.

I **(50)** .... we can see each other soon.

Daniel

PART 8

QUESTIONS 51–55

Read the advertisement and the email.

Fill in the information in Martina's notes.

For questions 51–55, write the information on your answer sheet.

Starlight Dance Studio

New term starts June 30th

Hip-Hop
Wednesday or Saturday
10 a.m. or 4 p.m.

Jazz Dance
Sunday or Thursday
11 a.m. or 5 p.m.

Mornings: £7
Afternoons: £9

From:	Nicole
To:	Martina

Martina, dance classes start again soon. We did Jazz Dance last term, so let's try Hip-Hop. I can't do weekdays because of work, and I'd prefer a morning class. Afternoon classes are more expensive anyway. Let's go by car, as it's not easy to get there by bus.

Martina's Notes
Dance classes with Nicole

Where:	Starlight Dance Studio
Type of dance:	**51**
Day of my class:	**52**
Time of class:	**53**
Travel there by:	**54**
Each class costs:	**55**

PART 9

QUESTION 56

Read this email from your friend, Jem.

From:	Jem
To:	

I heard you lost your school bag yesterday. Where did you last see it? What does it look like? What was in it?

Write an email to Jem and answer the questions.
Write 25–35 words.
Write the email on your answer sheet.

PAPER 2 LISTENING (approximately 30 minutes including 8 minutes transfer time)

PART 1

QUESTIONS 1–5

You will hear five short conversations.

You will hear each conversation twice.

There is one question for each conversation.

For questions 1–5, put a tick (✓) under the right answer.

Example:

0 How many people were at the meeting?

3	13	30
A ☐	B ☐	C ✓

---

1 Which T-shirt does the woman buy?

A ☐   B ☐   C ☐

2 When is the girl's swimming lesson next week?

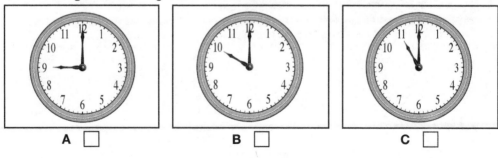

A ☐   B ☐   C ☐

3   Which bus stop does the woman need?

A ☐   B ☐   C ☐

4   Which is the man's raincoat?

A ☐   B ☐   C ☐

5   Which is the office manager?

   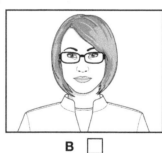   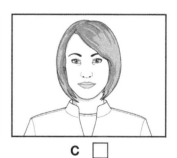

A ☐   B ☐   C ☐

PART 2

QUESTIONS 6–10

Listen to Amy and James talking about planning a birthday party.
What job is each person going to do?
For questions 6–10, write a letter A–H next to each person.
You will hear the conversation twice.

Example:

0   Chris   F

PEOPLE

6   Amy

7   James

8   Claire

9   Tom

10   Jane

JOBS

A   book the room

B   buy a present

C   buy party food

D   get drinks

E   invite guests

F   make cake

G   plan the music

H   put up balloons

PART 3

QUESTIONS 11–15

Listen to Jessica talking to Frank about a dance class.
For questions 11–15, tick (✓) A, B or C.
You will hear the conversation twice.

Example:

0	What time does the class start?	**A**	7.30 p.m.	☐
		B	8 p.m.	✓
		C	9 p.m.	☐

11	The class takes	**A**	half an hour.	☐
		B	three quarters of an hour.	☐
		C	an hour.	☐

12	What doesn't Frank need to take?	**A**	trainers	☐
		B	sports clothes	☐
		C	drink	☐

13	The teacher needs to know	**A**	if people are beginners.	☐
		B	how fit people are.	☐
		C	people's age.	☐

14 The normal price of classes is

    A £5. ☐

    B £6. ☑

    C £8. ☐

15 They will meet

    A at Jessica's house. ☐

    B at college. ☐

    C in the café. ☑

PART 4

QUESTIONS 16–20

You will hear a woman asking about a tour of a castle.
Listen and complete questions 16–20.
You will hear the conversation twice.

Castle Tours

Time of first tour:		10 a.m.
Tour takes:	**16**	.... minutes
Price of a family ticket:	**17**	£
Ticket includes:	**18**	soft drink or ....
Name of gardens:	**19**	
What to see in gardens:	**20**	800-year-old ....

PART 5

QUESTIONS 21–25

You will hear someone talking on the radio about a cooking programme.
Listen and complete questions 21–25.
You will hear the information twice.

New cooking programme

Name of programme:	Cooking for Beginners
Day of programme:	**21**
Start time:	**22** .... p.m.
Total number of shows:	**23**
Things to cook:	**24** cakes, main courses and ....
Date of first programme:	**25** July

You now have 8 minutes to write your answers on the answer sheet.

PAPER 3   SPEAKING (8–10 minutes)

The Speaking test lasts 8 to 10 minutes. You will take the test with another candidate. There are two examiners, but only one of them will talk to you. The examiner will ask you questions and ask you to talk to the other candidate.

Part 1 (5–6 minutes)

The examiner will ask you and your partner some questions. These questions will be about your daily life, past experience and future plans. For example, you may have to speak about your school, job, hobbies or home town.

Part 2 (3–4 minutes)

You and your partner will speak to each other. You will ask and answer questions. The examiner will give you a card with some information on it. The examiner will give your partner a card with some words on it. Your partner will use the words on the card to ask you questions about the information you have. Then you will change roles.

Test 2

PAPER 1 READING AND WRITING (1 hour 10 minutes)

PART 1

QUESTIONS 1–5

Which notice (A–H) says this (1–5)?
For questions 1–5, mark the correct letter A–H on your answer sheet.

Example:

0 It is not safe to do these things.

Answer:

	A	B	C	D	E	F	G	H
0	☐	☐	☐	☐	☐	☐	☐	■

---

1 For this price, you can get close to some animals.

A
> **Zoo shop**
> Great prices on all animal books

2 There are two ways to get information about this.

B
> **Meet the penguins!**
> 2p.m. / 6p.m.
> Only 6 tickets available for each time

C
> Spend a day with elephants or giraffes
> £85
> Adults only

3 This activity is for a small group of people.

D
> Monkey house closed
> until next June

4 This place isn't for adults or teenagers.

E
> Fish from South America
> Children – please do not hit the glass

5 It is not possible to see these animals today.

F
> Playground
> For children aged 3-11 only
> £2.50 per child

G
> **Birthday parties at the Zoo**
> For prices, visit reception or go online

H
> Standing or climbing on the zoo walls is dangerous

PART 2

QUESTIONS 6–10

Read the sentences about a girl who plays tennis.
Choose the best word (A, B or C) for each space.
For questions 6–10, mark A, B or C on your answer sheet.

Example:

0   Sharon has played tennis since she was a little girl and
      is now .... good.

   A   nearly   **B**   possibly   **C**   quite   *Answer:* | 0 | A B C ■ |

---

6   Sharon .... at her tennis club four times a week.

   A   joins   **B**   enjoys   **C**   practises

7   Sharon .... lots of competitions and often plays very well in them.

   A   enters   **B**   takes   **C**   earns

8   It's Sharon's birthday soon and she has .... her parents for a new racket.

   A   told   **B**   asked   **C**   spoken

9   When Sharon loses a match, she always feels very ....

   A   upset   **B**   difficult   **C**   worst

10   Sharon's friend has just started playing tennis and Sharon is helping her to ....

   A   copy   **B**   improve   **C**   know

PART 3

QUESTIONS 11–15

Complete the five conversations.
For questions 11–15, mark A, B or C on your answer sheet.

Example:

0

Where do you come from?

A New York.

B School.

C Home.

Answer:

0	A	B	C
	■	☐	☐

---

11 How did you get to the party?

A I caught a bus.

B It was great thanks.

C On Wednesday I think.

12 Yuri phoned me yesterday from Japan.

A Who's calling?

B How is she?

C Can I leave a message?

13 Is that Stella's new mobile?

A I can't find one.

B She didn't answer.

C She hasn't bought one yet.

14 I'm going clothes shopping tomorrow.

A Are they in the town centre?

B How long is it?

C What do you need to get?

15 The library's closed already.

A It's a pity you can't.

B I can wait until tomorrow.

C Can I borrow it?

QUESTIONS 16–20

Complete the conversation.

What does Sarah say to Alice?

For questions 16–20, mark the correct letter A–H on your answer sheet.

Example:

Alice: Hi Sarah, are you going to Grace's party tomorrow?

Sarah: 0 ....**H**...............

Answer:

	A	B	C	D	E	F	G	H
0	☐	☐	☐	☐	☐	☐	☐	■

Alice: Oh, come on! It'll be fun.

Sarah: **16** ....

Alice: I'm driving, and there's still space in my car.

Sarah: **17** ....

Alice: I've bought one – we can say it's from both of us.

Sarah: **18** ....

Alice: Great – I'll write my name on it. Shall I pick you up at 7 o'clock?

Sarah: **19** ....

Alice: Of course! By the way, I can't stay too late at the party.

Sarah: **20** ....

Alice: Me too!

A   No problem – I have to work the next day anyway.

B   That's fine. You know the way to my house, don't you?

C   How many people are going to be there?

D   Oh, OK then. How are you getting there?

E   Great, I'll go with you, then. What about a present?

F   It's quite an expensive one.

G   Thanks. I'll give you some money for that, and I'll get a card.

H   I haven't decided yet.

PART 4

QUESTIONS 21–27

**Read the article about the bedrooms of three teenagers and then answer
the questions.**
For questions 21–27, mark A, B or C on your answer sheet.

My Bedroom

Robert

Robert likes his room to be tidy, but it's difficult as it's his brother's bedroom
too. When Robert is alone in the room he does his homework or listens
to music. On the walls there are a few small posters. Robert wants to have
more, and to paint the walls yellow, but his mother doesn't agree. There are
photographs of family holidays and of his sister's children. 'I like my room
best when they're here. It gets untidy, but I don't mind.'

James

James's bedroom is painted in his favourite colour, yellow. He loves rugby, and
there are several photos of him playing in the school team. 'After school I like
to come up here to play computer games. My room's like my safe place. I can
relax here.' James keeps his room tidy. His school work is on one shelf, and on
another he has all his books.

Harry

'After school I come up here and chat to everyone I know on the computer,'
says Harry. 'I never work in here – I study in the kitchen.' He has a big desk
with a laptop in the middle, a PC on one side and a lamp on the other. On the
walls there are two posters of his favourite tennis stars. 'I don't do much sport
but I like watching tennis.'

Example:

0   Whose room has yellow walls?

   A   Robert's   **B**   James's   **C**   Harry's

Answer:

---

21   Who has more than one computer in his room.

   A   Robert   **B**   James   **C**   Harry

22   Who would like more pictures on the walls?

   A   Robert   **B**   James   **C**   Harry

23   Who has pictures of himself doing sport?

   A   Robert   **B**   James   **C**   Harry

24   Who shares his room with someone else?

   A   Robert   **B**   James   **C**   Harry

25   Who talks to friends when he's in his room?

   A   Robert   **B**   James   **C**   Harry

26   Who sometimes has visitors to his room?

   A   Robert   **B**   James   **C**   Harry

27   Who studies in his bedroom?

   A   Robert   **B**   James   **C**   Harry

PART 5

QUESTIONS 28–35

Read the article about cheetahs.
Choose the best word (A, B or C) for each space.
For questions 28–35, mark A, B or C on your answer sheet.

Cheetahs

Most wild cheetahs **(0)** .... found in eastern and
south-western Africa. When running, they can go
from 0 to 100 kilometres an hour **(28)** .... only
three seconds. They can't run this **(29)** .... for
very long, however, and usually stop **(30)** ....
about a minute. Cheetahs can also see very well,
(31) .... is useful when they are **(32)** .... to
catch small animals.

Female cheetahs usually have three cubs at a time. These stay with their
mother for between one and a half to two years. They spend most of this
time playing together or learning **(33)** .... to catch small animals. Male
cheetahs live alone or in small groups, **(34)** .... with their brothers.
Cheetahs are not as big as other members **(35)** .... the cat family, such as
lions or tigers, and only weigh 45–60 kilograms.

Example:

0	**A** is	**B** has	**C** are			

Answer: 0   A B C ☐☐■

---

28 **A** on   **B** in   **C** at

29 **A** fast   **B** faster   **C** fastest

30 **A** after   **B** until   **C** during

31 **A** who   **B** where   **C** which

32 **A** try   **B** trying   **C** tried

33 **A** ever   **B** yet   **C** how

34 **A** already   **B** exactly   **C** often

35 **A** of   **B** by   **C** to

PART 6

QUESTIONS 36–40

Read the descriptions of some travel words.
What is the word for each one?
The first letter is already there. There is one space for each other letter in the word.
For questions 36–40, write the words on your answer sheet.

Example:

0 You need to buy this before you travel on a bus or train.   **t** __ __ __ __ __

                                                 Answer: | **0** | *ticket* |

---

36 You go on this when you fly from one place to another.   **p** __ __ __ __

37 You go to this place when you need to catch a train or coach.   **s** __ __ __ __ __ __ __

38 When you arrive in a new country, you may have to show this.   **p** __ __ __ __ __ __ __

39 If you look at this, it will help you find your way around a new city.   **m** __ __

40 You arrive here when you fly into another country.   **a** __ __ __ __ __ __ __

PART 7

QUESTIONS 41–50

Complete the email.
Write **ONE** word for each space.
For questions 41–50, write the words on your answer sheet.

Example: **0**   y o u

From:	Parveen
To:	Marta

Hi Marta,

I hope **(0)** .... are well. I was trying **(41)** .... call you yesterday but you didn't answer. Is your phone broken, **(42)** .... have you lost it again? Anyway, I wanted to ask **(43)** .... you can come to my birthday party next Saturday. My birthday was actually two weeks **(44)** .... , but I couldn't have the party then **(45)** .... lots of people were **(46)** .... holiday.

I've invited **(47)** .... few people from our swimming club, as well as my friends from school. **(48)** .... you think your brother **(49)** .... free that day? Please invite **(50)** .... to come too. The party's at my house and starts at 8 p.m.

Parveen

PART 8

QUESTIONS 51–55

Read the advertisement and the email.

Fill in the information in Lin's notes.

For questions 51–55, write the information on your answer sheet.

REDWOOD CINEMA

Special showings this weekend

Rosy's Story:	Saturday 8 p.m.
	Sunday 3 p.m.
Storm:	Saturday 9 p.m.
	Sunday 7 p.m.

Adults: £8.00
Students/Children: £5.00

From: Ines
To: Lin

My sister's visiting this weekend, so there'll be three of us going to the cinema instead of two. I've already seen *Storm*, so let's see the other film. Let's go in the evening, because we need to study during the day. Could you buy the tickets, as you live nearer? Don't forget to show your university ID so we get in cheaper.

Lin's notes
Cinema this weekend

Cinema:	Redwood
Film:	**51**
Day:	**52**
Time:	**53** p.m.
Number of tickets to get:	**54**
Price per person:	**55** £

46

PART 9

QUESTION 56

You are planning a picnic for next Saturday.
Write an email to your English friend, Charley:

- invite Charley to come

- say where Charley should meet you

- tell Charley what to bring

Write an email to Charley.
Write 25–35 words.
Write the email on your answer sheet.

PAPER 2   LISTENING (approximately 30 minutes including 8 minutes transfer time)

PART 1

QUESTIONS 1–5

You will hear five short conversations.

You will hear each conversation twice.

There is one question for each conversation.

For questions 1–5, put a tick (✓) under the right answer.

Example:

0   How many people were at the meeting?

3	13	30
A ☐	B ☐	C ✓

---

1   What does the woman order?

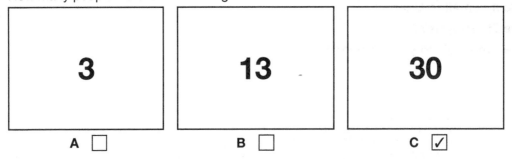

A ☐   B ☐   C ☐

2   What size boots is the woman going to try on next?

A ☐   B ☐   C ☐

3   Where will the man get off the bus?

A ☐   B ☐   C ☑

4   How many books does the boy want to borrow now?

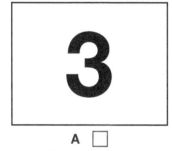   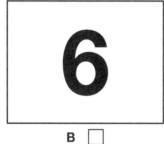   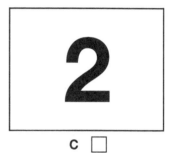

A ☐   B ☐   C ☐

5   What job does Mark's brother do?

A ☐   B ☐   C ☐

PART 2

QUESTIONS 6–10

Listen to Emily and John talking about activities they did last weekend.
Which activity did each person do?
For questions 6–10, write a letter A–H next to each person.
You will hear the conversation twice.

Example:

0   John | C |

PEOPLE		ACTIVITIES
6 Pete	☐	**A** basketball
		B cycling
7 Emily	☐	
		C fishing
8 Jenny	☐	**D** football
9 Joe	☐	**E** skateboarding
		F swimming
10 Andy	☐	**G** table-tennis
		H tennis

PART 3

QUESTIONS 11–15

Listen to Suzy talking to a friend about a new shop.
For questions 11–15, tick (✓) A, B or C.
You will hear the conversation twice.

Example:

0	When did the new shop open?	**A**	today	☐
		B	yesterday	☐
		C	last week	✓

11	Where is the new shop?	**A**	near the college	☐
		B	outside the town centre	☐
		C	opposite the newsagent's	☐

12	In the shop you cannot buy	**A**	clothes.	☐
		B	bags.	☐
		C	boots.	☐

13	What time does the shop close on a Thursday?	**A**	6 p.m.	☐
		B	8 p.m.	☐
		C	10 p.m.	☐

14 What days does the shop open?

    A Tuesday to Sunday ☐

    B every day ☐

    C Monday to Friday ☐

15 What should Suzy's friend do if she wants a job?

    A phone the manager ☐

    B go to the shop ☐

    C write a letter ☐

PART 4

QUESTIONS 16–20

You will hear a man phoning about a flat he wants to rent.
Listen and complete questions 16–20.
You will hear the conversation twice.

Flat to rent

Address of flat:	25A Green Street
Price of flat:	**16** £............................... a month
How far from station:	**17** .... minutes on foot
Number of bedrooms:	**18**
Furniture in flat:	**19** .... and table
Day to see flat:	**20**

PART 5

QUESTIONS 21–25

You will hear some information for new students about a college.
Listen and complete questions 21–25.
You will hear the information twice.

Langley College

Day classes start: Wednesday

Cost to join sports centre per year:
21 £ ....

Closing time of café:
22 .... p.m.

Name of receptionist:
23 Mrs ....

Phone number:
24

What to bring to college:
25

You now have 8 minutes to write your answers on the answer sheet.

PAPER 3 SPEAKING (8–10 minutes)

The Speaking test lasts 8 to 10 minutes. You will take the test with another candidate. There are two examiners, but only one of them will talk to you. The examiner will ask you questions and ask you to talk to the other candidate.

Part 1 (5–6 minutes)

The examiner will ask you and your partner some questions. These questions will be about your daily life, past experience and future plans. For example, you may have to speak about your school, job, hobbies or home town.

Part 2 (3–4 minutes)

You and your partner will speak to each other. You will ask and answer questions. The examiner will give you a card with some information on it. The examiner will give your partner a card with some words on it. Your partner will use the words on the card to ask you questions about the information you have. Then you will change roles.

Test 3

PAPER 1 READING AND WRITING (1 hour 10 minutes)

PART 1

QUESTIONS 1–5

Which notice (A–H) says this (1–5)?
For questions 1–5, mark the correct letter A–H on your answer sheet.

Example:

0 There is no cost to leave your car here if you use a shop.

Answer:

0	A	B	C	D	E	F	G	H
	☐	☐	■	☐	☐	☐	☐	☐

---

1 You shouldn't go in through the front entrance of the shop.

A This month only – 60% discount on all pet care magazines

B Special offer! Free toy with every box of dog food

2 Extra staff are needed here for weekend work.

C Animal World Free parking for customers (Monday – Saturday)

D Pete's Pets 8 a.m. - 6 p.m. weekdays 8 a.m. - midday weekends

3 Please ask the shop assistants if you need any help.

E Wanted – Sales Assistants Saturday to Sunday 11 a.m. – 6 p.m. £6 per hour

4 You cannot buy a pet here on Saturday or Sunday afternoon.

F Japanese goldfish for sale £5 each

G ALL CUSTOMERS DURING BUILDING WORK USE SIDE DOOR ONLY

5 These are cheaper at the moment.

H Bags of animal food too heavy? Our staff will carry them for you

PART 2

QUESTIONS 6–10

Read the sentences about going to a restaurant.
Choose the best word (A, B or C) for each space.
For questions 6–10, mark A, B or C on your answer
sheet.

Example:

0   Joe and his friends often go to their .... pizza restaurant in town.

    A   great   **B**   lovely   **C**   favourite   *Answer:*

	A	B	C
0	☐	☐	■

---

6   Joe enjoys .... different dishes on the menu.

    A   doing   **B**   trying   **C**   using

7   The pizza restaurant is often .... of people at the weekends.

    A   busy   **B**   crowded   **C**   full

8   The waiters at the restaurant are really .... to their customers.

    A   fast   **B**   friendly   **C**   careful

9   Joe and his friends often share a pizza, so the meal doesn't .... too much.

    A   cost   **B**   spend   **C**   pay

10   Joe thinks he would .... to work in a restaurant when he is older.

    A   like   **B**   want   **C**   decide

PART 3

QUESTIONS 11–15

Complete the five conversations.
For questions 11–15, mark A, B or C on your answer sheet.

Example:

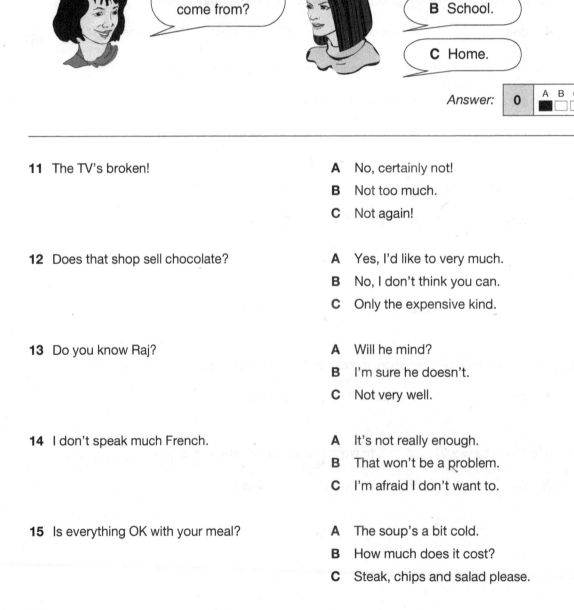

0

Where do you come from?

A New York.

B School.

C Home.

Answer: **0** A B C

---

11 The TV's broken!

A   No, certainly not!

B   Not too much.

C   Not again!

12 Does that shop sell chocolate?

A   Yes, I'd like to very much.

B   No, I don't think you can.

C   Only the expensive kind.

13 Do you know Raj?

A   Will he mind?

B   I'm sure he doesn't.

C   Not very well.

14 I don't speak much French.

A   It's not really enough.

B   That won't be a problem.

C   I'm afraid I don't want to.

15 Is everything OK with your meal?

A   The soup's a bit cold.

B   How much does it cost?

C   Steak, chips and salad please.

QUESTIONS 16–20

Complete the conversation.
What does Xavier say to Toby?
For questions 16–20, mark the correct letter A–H on your answer sheet.

Example:

Toby:	Hi, Xavier. It's Toby here.

Xavier: **0** .... **D** ....   *Answer:*

0	A B C D E F G H ☐☐☐■☐☐☐☐

Toby:	I'm fine, thanks. Listen, do you know about the new guitar lessons at school?		**A**	Maybe we'll be better!
Xavier:	**16**		**B**	Yes. Shall I ask the teacher?
Toby:	Well, I might, but I'll have to find out the cost of the instrument and lessons first.		**C**	Me too. Wasn't your father in one with his friends?
Xavier:	**17**			
Toby:	Really? Do you know why that is?		**D**	Hi Toby. How are you?
			E	Yes. Are you going to do them?
Xavier:	**18**			
Toby:	That sounds great! I've always wanted to be in a band.		**F**	My friend Susie is a really good singer.
Xavier:	**19**		**G**	They want to make sure we are interested before we start paying.
Toby:	Yes, but I don't think they were very good.			
Xavier:	**20**		**H**	I think the teacher said they are free the first term.
Toby:	I'm sure you're right!			

PART 4

QUESTIONS 21–27

Read the article about Erden Eruç, a famous explorer.
Are sentences 21–27 'Right' (A) or 'Wrong' (B)?
If there is not enough information to answer 'Right' (A) or 'Wrong' (B), choose
'Doesn't say' (C).
For questions 21–27, mark A, B or C on your answer sheet.

An Amazing Adventure

Erden Eruç is Turkish but now lives in Seattle, USA, with his wife Nancy. In July 2012, he completed an amazing 5-year journey, becoming the first person ever to travel all the way around the world with no help from engines or sails. All he used were his own arms and legs, to cycle, row, and walk around the world.

His plan before beginning the trip was to climb the highest mountain on each of the six continents that he went through. Unfortunately he was only able to climb three of them because of bad weather and money problems.

Erden spent a lot of his time on the trip rowing his boat. His journey across the Pacific Ocean took 312 days. Being alone for that much time was not at all easy, but he kept busy by listening to music and studying Spanish. He took dried food with him and had a water machine to make fresh water out of seawater. However, it only worked on sunny days.

Erden is sure he will have more adventures one day. But at the moment all he wants to do is rest, think about his trip and spend time with Nancy.

Example:

0   Erden Eruç comes from Turkey.

A   Right   **B**   Wrong   **C**   Doesn't say   *Answer:*   ☐ 0   A B C ▨☐☐

---

21   Erden began his journey around the world in 2012.

A   Right   **B**   Wrong   **C**   Doesn't say

22   Erden travelled around the world by bike, boat and on foot.

A   Right   **B**   Wrong   **C**   Doesn't say

23   The plan to climb the mountains was made after Erden started the journey.

A   Right   **B**   Wrong   **C**   Doesn't say

24   It was difficult for Erden to be by himself for so long while he was rowing.

A   Right   **B**   Wrong   **C**   Doesn't say

25   Erden already spoke a little Spanish before he began his trip.

A   Right   **B**   Wrong   **C**   Doesn't say

26   Erden was able to use his water machine every day.

A   Right   **B**   Wrong   **C**   Doesn't say

27   As soon as he returned, Erden began planning his next adventure.

A   Right   **B**   Wrong   **C**   Doesn't say

PART 5

QUESTIONS 28–35

Read the article about African elephants.
Choose the best word (A, B or C) for each space.
For questions 28–35, mark A, B or C on your answer sheet.

The African Elephant

African elephants are the **(0)** .... land animals
on earth. They live together in family groups
and move from place **(28)** .... place looking
for food and water. They do not sleep **(29)** .... and can walk an amazing
80km without **(30)** .... a rest. Adult elephants eat up to 130kg of food a
day. They eat plants of almost any size, from grass to trees.

Elephants must have water for cleaning **(31)** .... as well as for drinking,
(32) .... they prefer to live as close to rivers and lakes as possible.
Female elephants have a baby **(33)** .... four years. Other elephants in
(34) .... same group help the females to look after the babies. This shows
(35) .... family groups are very important for these wonderful animals.

Example:

| 0 | **A** large | **B** larger | **C** largest | *Answer:* | 0 | A B C ☐☐■ |

---

28 **A** at   **B** to   **C** by

29 **A** much   **B** more   **C** most

30 **A** need   **B** needed   **C** needing

31 **A** themselves   **B** yourselves   **C** ourselves

32 **A** except   **B** if   **C** so

33 **A** every   **B** all   **C** each

34 **A** a   **B** the   **C** one

35 **A** what   **B** which   **C** that

PART 6

QUESTIONS 36–40

Read the descriptions of some words about shopping.
What is the word for each one?
The first letter is already there. There is one space for each other letter in the word.
For questions 36–40, write the words on your answer sheet.

Example:

0   This person works in a shop and can help you find what
you need.   **a** __ __ __ __ __ __ __ __

Answer: **0**   a s s i s t a n t

---

36   This is often made of leather and men keep their money in it.   **w** __ __ __ __ __

37   You may go here to get some cash before you go shopping.   **b** __ __ __

38   If you need medicine, you can buy it at this shop.   **c** __ __ __ __ __ __

39   If you are tired after shopping, you can have something to
eat or drink here.   **c** __ __ __

40   After shopping, you may catch this to go home.   **b** __ __

PART 7

QUESTIONS 41–50

Complete the email.
Write ONE word for each space.
For questions 41–50, write the words on your answer sheet.

Example: | **0** | *t o* |

From:	Conny
To:	Marcia

Hi Marcia,

Do you remember I wanted **(0)** .... invite you, Sasha and John to my new house? Well, **(41)** .... about next Saturday evening? We **(42)** .... a beautiful garden with lots **(43)** .... trees. We may have a barbeque outside **(44)** .... it doesn't rain. My mother is **(45)** .... really good cook and I **(46)** .... going to help her make the food.

Afterwards, **(47)** .... don't we watch a film? **(48)** .... you bring a DVD with you as I haven't got many here?

John's coming **(49)** .... bike and Sasha is getting a lift **(50)** .... her father. I hope you'll be able to come too.

Let me know soon!

Conny

PART 8

QUESTIONS 51–55

Read the notice and the email.

Fill in the information in Paulo's notes.

For questions 51–55, write the information on your answer sheet.

Liston Sports Centre

After-school swimming lessons
4 p.m. to 5 p.m. daily

*Tom is teaching the over 18s this term so
Julie is teaching these classes:*

Level	Day
1	Monday
2	Tuesday
3	Wednesday
4	Thursday
5	Friday

Prices:
Ages	11–14	£65
	15–18	£85

From:	Suli
To:	Paulo

Thanks for booking our swimming lessons! We were level 3 last term so we'll be level 4 now, and we've both turned 15, which means it's a bit more expensive. Don't forget Lena can't come this time, so there'll be two of us instead of three.

Paulo's Notes
Swimming Course

Place:	Liston Sports Centre
Time lesson starts:	**51** _____ p.m.
Price:	**52** £ _____
Day:	**53** _____
Name of our teacher:	**54** _____
Number of people:	**55** _____

PART 9

QUESTION 56

Read this email from your English friend Sami.

From:	Sami
To:	

Please tell me about the concert next Friday. Where is it? What time does it start? How are we going to get there?

Write an email to Sami and answer the questions.
Write 25–35 words.
Write the email on your answer sheet.

PAPER 2   LISTENING (approximately 30 minutes including 8 minutes transfer time)

PART 1

QUESTIONS 1–5

You will hear five short conversations.

You will hear each conversation twice.

There is one question for each conversation.

For questions 1–5, put a tick (✓) under the right answer.

Example:

0   How many people were at the meeting?

3	**13**	**30**
A ☐	B ☐	C ✓

---

1   What instrument is Edward learning to play?

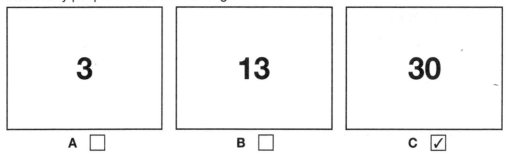

A ☐   B ☐   C ☐

2   What will Anna have for breakfast today?

A ☐   B ☐   C ☐

3   How much is the watch?

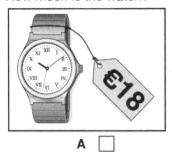

A ☐

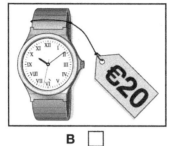

B ☐

C ☐

4   What does Mandy's brother do?

A ☐

B ☐

C ☐

5   Who is coming to stay this weekend?

A ☐

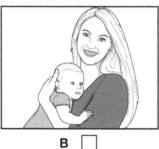

B ☐

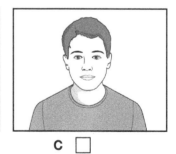

C ☐

PART 2

QUESTIONS 6–10

Listen to the conversation between Sally and her father about a computer course.
How many free places are there on the computer course each day?
For questions 6–10, write a letter A–H next to each day.
You will hear the conversation twice.

Example:

0 Monday   **D**

DAYS   **NUMBER OF FREE PLACES**

6 Tuesday   **A** none

7 Wednesday   **B** one

                                            C two

8 Thursday   **D** three

9 Friday   **E** four

                                            F five

10 Saturday   **G** six

                                            H seven

PART 3

QUESTIONS 11–15

Listen to Stephen talking to Jenny about making some soup.
For questions 11–15, tick (✓) A, B or C.
You will hear the conversation twice.

Example:

0	To make the soup, Jenny uses	**A**	roast tomatoes.	☐
		B	fresh tomatoes.	☐
		C	a can of tomatoes.	✓

11	Jenny was shown how to make the soup by	**A**	her aunt.	☐
		B	her friend.	☐
		C	her mother.	☐

12	How has Jenny improved the soup?	**A**	She adds less water.	☐
		B	She makes it thinner.	☐
		C	She uses bigger cups.	☐

13	To make it really good, Jenny adds	**A**	milk.	☐
		B	butter.	☐
		C	cream.	☐

14 How long does the soup take to make?

    A   about 5 minutes   ☐

    B   about 10 minutes   ☐

    C   about 20 minutes   ☐

15 What will they eat next?

    A   fruit cake   ☐

    B   pasta   ☐

    C   lemon chicken   ☐

PART 4

QUESTIONS 16–20

You will hear a boy asking for information about a plant.
Listen and complete questions 16–20.
You will hear the conversation twice.

Plant for Mum

Name of plant:	*Sweet William*
Colour of flowers:	**16**
Season to see flowers:	**17**
Month to put plant outside:	**18**
Final size of plant:	**19** .... cm tall
Price of plant today:	**20** £ ....

PART 5

QUESTIONS 21–25

You will hear some information about a day trip.
Listen and complete questions 21–25.
You will hear the information twice.

Day trip to the lake

Name of lake:	North Lake
Travel there by:	**21**
Time to meet:	**22** .... p.m.
Activities:	**23** walking and ....
How much money to take:	**24** £
Meet at end of day at:	**25** the .... Hotel

You now have 8 minutes to write your answers on the answer sheet.

PAPER 3 SPEAKING (8–10 minutes)

The Speaking test lasts 8 to 10 minutes. You will take the test with another candidate. There are two examiners, but only one of them will talk to you. The examiner will ask you questions and ask you to talk to the other candidate.

Part 1 (5–6 minutes)

The examiner will ask you and your partner some questions. These questions will be about your daily life, past experience and future plans. For example, you may have to speak about your school, job, hobbies or home town.

Part 2 (3–4 minutes)

You and your partner will speak to each other. You will ask and answer questions. The examiner will give you a card with some information on it. The examiner will give your partner a card with some words on it. Your partner will use the words on the card to ask you questions about the information you have. Then you will change roles.

Test 4

PAPER 1 READING AND WRITING (1 hour 10 minutes)

PART 1

QUESTIONS 1–5

Which notice (A–H) says this (1–5)?
For questions 1–5, mark the correct letter A–H on your answer sheet.

Example:

0   You can't pay by card.

Answer:

	0	A	B	C	D	E	F	G	H
		□	□	□	□	□	□	□	■

---

1   This is cheaper than usual if you buy something else.

A

> Arabic and French dictionaries for sale
> Great prices!
> Contact David

B

> **Student café**
> Hot meals served until 10 p.m.
> everyday

2   If you become a member, you will get a discount.

C

> Learning Centre
> Every student can borrow up to 3 books

D

> **Closed for cleaning**
> Please use toilets upstairs
> near the café.

3   If you want to buy a book, speak to this person.

E

> With every coffee,
> get a sandwich for £1!
> (normal price £2.50)

4   This place is open in the evenings.

F

> **Football practice**
> Wednesday 7 p.m. – 8 p.m.
> Call Bryan on 0489 967622

G

> College Gym
> Join now for 12 months and only
> pay for 10

5   You cannot enter here at the moment.

H

> **College Café**
> Sorry, cash only — no credit cards

PART 2

QUESTIONS 6–10

Read the sentences about going to the theatre.
Choose the best word (A, B or C) for each space.
For questions 6–10, mark A, B or C on your answer
sheet.

Example:

0   Helen .... to go to the theatre with a friend.

    A   enjoyed   **B**   thought   **C**   wanted   *Answer:*

0	A	B	C
	☐	☐	■

---

6   She .... her friend Sarah if she would like to go too.

    A   said   **B**   told   **C**   asked

7   Helen called the theatre and .... two tickets.

    A   paid   **B**   booked   **C**   offered

8   She chose some .... near the stage.

    A   seats   **B**   chairs   **C**   sofas

9   At the theatre Helen and Sarah went to the café for a drink and a .... of cake.

    A   cup   **B**   part   **C**   slice

10   They had a good .... of the stage from where they sat.

    A   view   **B**   way   **C**   place

PART 3

QUESTIONS 11–15

Complete the five conversations.
For questions 11–15, mark A, B or C on your answer sheet.

Example:

0

Where do you come from?	**A** New York.
	B School.
	C Home.

Answer: 0 A B C ■□□

---

11 Don't forget to buy some fresh bread on your way home.

A Not at all.
B I hope so.
C I'll try not to.

12 Can you help me with my homework?

A How do you know about that?
B How long is it going to take?
C How often do you go there?

13 Remember to take your keys with you.

A I've got them already.
B I haven't been there yet.
C They're going out now.

14 We have to turn left at the next traffic lights.

A Not very often.
B I don't agree.
C It's not much.

15 Who's our maths teacher this year?

A I don't think so.
B No one's told us yet.
C He doesn't like it.

QUESTIONS 16–20

Complete the conversation between two friends.
What does Danika say to Lisa?
For questions 16–20, mark the correct letter A–H on your answer sheet.

Example:

Lisa:	Are you busy this Saturday?
Danika:	0 ....**D**..............

Answer:

0	A	B	C	D	E	F	G	H
	☐	☐	☐	■	☐	☐	☐	☐

Lisa: Would you like to go to a concert?

Danika: 16 ....

Lisa: Well, 'Rex' are playing in town this weekend.

Danika: 17 ....

Lisa: Lots of times! You should listen to them online before we go.

Danika: 18 ....

Lisa: We'll need to. Lots of people will want to go. I can get them on Wednesday.

Danika: 19 ....

Lisa: Great. Shall I meet you at the bus station on Saturday at about 8 p.m.?

Danika: 20 ....

Lisa: Sure, no problem. It will be awesome!

A Can we make it half an hour earlier?

B Alright. I'll give you the money tomorrow.

C Have you seen them before?

D No, I'm not doing anything. Why?

E Are they playing at the same time on Sunday?

F That sounds like a great idea! Who do you want to see?

G OK, I'll do that. Shall we book tickets?

H It's not too expensive, is it?

PART 4

QUESTIONS 21–27

Read the article about a teenage rower.

Are sentences 21–27 'Right' (A) or 'Wrong' (B)?

If there is not enough information to answer 'Right' (A) or 'Wrong' (B), choose 'Doesn't say' (C).

For questions 21–27, mark A, B or C on your answer sheet.

David Rawson

David Rawson, 15, is one of the best rowers of his age in the USA. He comes from Connecticut, and spends most of his free time practising on the many rivers near his home.

David's dad Martin also enjoys rowing. 'David's much better than me, but I go with him when I can,' he says. David's mother, Wendy, doesn't go rowing herself but she is happy to take them to and from the rivers in her car.

It's an expensive sport. The Rawsons have seven boats, costing between $1500 and $4000 each. But you can see how important rowing is to the family when you go to their home. There are many photos of David rowing and several rowing boats in the garage.

About 18 months ago, David started rowing on the sea. This sport is similar to surfing except that you sit in a special boat instead of standing on a board. David loves it, and it means he can continue with his sport in the summer when his favourite rivers don't have enough water in them.

Next year David is hoping to go to the Premier Rowing Academy where he'll study rowing as well as all the usual school subjects.

Example:

0   David Rawson is better than most other rowers of his age in his country.

A   Right   **B**   Wrong   **C**   Doesn't say   *Answer:* | 0 | A B C |

---

21   There are lots of places for David to do his sport in his area.

A   Right   **B**   Wrong   **C**   Doesn't say

22   Martin says that David is nearly as good at rowing as him.

A   Right   **B**   Wrong   **C**   Doesn't say

23   Wendy helps Martin and David by doing the driving.

A   Right   **B**   Wrong   **C**   Doesn't say

24   The Rawsons paid the same price for all their boats.

A   Right   **B**   Wrong   **C**   Doesn't say

25   Wendy is unhappy about how many boats there are in the garage.

A   Right   **B**   Wrong   **C**   Doesn't say

26   David found a teacher to help him learn to row on the sea.

A   Right   **B**   Wrong   **C**   Doesn't say

27   It is possible for David to row on his favourite rivers all year.

A   Right   **B**   Wrong   **C**   Doesn't say

PART 5

QUESTIONS 28–35

Read the article about Emperor penguins.
Choose the best word (A, B or C) for each space.
For questions 28–35, mark A, B or C on your answer sheet.

Emperor Penguins

There are seventeen kinds of penguin **(0)** .... the world. Emperor penguins are the **(28)** .... of them all. They spend **(29)** .... lives in the Antarctic and are the only animals to stay there **(30)** .... the winter. Other animals find it **(31)** .... cold.

The female Emperor penguin lays one egg a year in winter. Then she leaves to go and **(32)** .... fish. The male keeps the egg with him on the ice. He **(33)** .... to keep it warm. He does this by putting it on his feet.

He looks after the egg **(34)** .... the baby penguin comes out, **(35)** .... usually takes about 65 days. Around that time, the female Emperor penguin returns to look after the baby chick. The hungry male can finally go into the sea to eat some fish.

Example:

0	**A** in	**B** on	**C** at	*Answer:*

0 ■ A □ B □ C

---

28 **A** large **B** larger **C** largest

29 **A** your **B** their **C** its

30 **A** since **B** from **C** during

31 **A** too **B** enough **C** even

32 **A** caught **B** catch **C** catching

33 **A** has **B** can **C** should

34 **A** by **B** until **C** to

35 **A** which **B** what **C** where

PART 6

QUESTIONS 36–40

Read the descriptions of some words about a birthday party.
What is the word for each one?
The first letter is already there. There is one space for each other letter in the word.
For questions 36–40, write the words on your answer sheet.

Example:

0   You listen to this when you dance.   m __ __ __ __

                                    Answer: | 0 | m u s i c |

---

36   You are often given lots of these on your birthday.   p __ __ __ __ __ __ __

37   A girl may wear this to a party.   d __ __ __ __ __

38   This drink is made from fruit and is often served at parties.   j __ __ __ __

39   At a children's party, people often play these.   g __ __ __ __ __

40   You write a message in this and give it to someone on their birthday.   c __ __ __ __

PART 7

QUESTIONS 41–50

Complete the email.

Write ONE word for each space.

For questions 41–50, write the words on your answer sheet.

Example:

0	in

From:	Rosario
To:	Melissa

Dear Melissa

How are things **(0)** .... London? I had a great time staying with you.
Thank you for looking after **(41)** .... You are **(42)** .... great cook
and your family were really kind to me. And my English is much better now
(43) .... it was before.

My flight home was fine – there were **(44)** .... delays at all. It's good to be
back, but I miss you all very **(45)** .... !

(46) .... you remember my friend Jenny? I think she came **(47)** ....
visit me at your house once **(48)** .... twice. Well, she took some great
photos **(49)** .... us on our last day at the language school. I'm sending
you one with this email. I hope you like **(50)** ....

Rosario

PART 8

QUESTIONS 51–55

Read the advertisement and the email.

Fill in the information in Sophie's notes.

For questions 51–55, write the information on your answer sheet.

Hill's bookshop
Just arrived!

'Better Photos', by David Fox,
writer of last year's best-selling book
'Learn Photography'

Usual price – £15.00
Buy here for £12.50

'This book's great!' – said fashion
photographer Jonny Clarke.

From:	Ben
To:	Sophie

My mum wants David Fox's latest book for her birthday. Can you get it from the bookshop near you because it's cheaper there? Her birthday's on June 11, so I need it on June 10 please. If there's a problem, call me at the office on 786 861. My new mobile number is 07920 3449.

Sophie's Notes
Trip to bookshop

Name of bookshop:	Hill's bookshop
Name of book to buy:	**51**
Price I'll pay:	**52** £
Writer of book:	**53**
Ben's work number:	**54**
Date Ben wants the book:	**55**

PART 9

QUESTION 56

You are on holiday. Write a postcard to your English friend, Jo:

- tell Jo what you did yesterday

- describe the weather

- say when you are coming home

Write a postcard to Jo.
Write 25–35 words.
Write the postcard on your answer sheet.

PAPER 2   LISTENING (approximately 30 minutes including 8 minutes transfer time)

PART 1

QUESTIONS 1–5

You will hear five short conversations.

You will hear each conversation twice.

There is one question for each conversation.

For questions 1–5, put a tick (✓) under the right answer.

Example:

0   How many people were at the meeting?

3	13	30
A ☐	B ☐	C ✓

---

1   How will they travel to the pop concert?

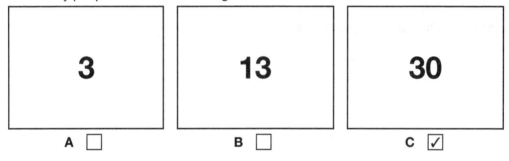

A ☐   B ☐   C ☐

2   What was the weather like on Beth's holiday?

A ☐   B ☐   C ☐

3   Where has the teacher put the dictionaries?

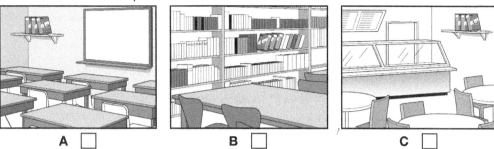

A ☐   B ☐   C ☐

4   Where did Paul go running yesterday?

A ☐   B ☐   C ☐

5   What does Karen still need to get for the school play?

A ☐   B ☐   C ☐

PART 2

QUESTIONS 6–10

Listen to Gemma telling a friend about her visits to different countries.
What did she like most about each country?
For questions 6–10, write a letter A–H next to each country.
You will hear the conversation twice.

Example:

0	France	H

COUNTRIES

6 Italy

7 Mexico

8 India

9 Australia

10 Canada

FAVOURITE THINGS

A animals

B beach

C countryside

D food

E hotel

F shops

G sport

H weather

PART 3

QUESTIONS 11–15

Listen to Tony talking to Lisa about a science club competition.
For questions 11–15, tick (✓) A, B or C.
You will hear the conversation twice.

Example:

0	Tony says the competition is on	**A**	Monday.	☐
		B	Tuesday.	☐
		C	Wednesday.	☑

11	Which building will the competition be in?	**A**	the school	☐
		B	the town hall	☐
		C	the university	☐
12	How has the team decided to get there?	**A**	They will catch a bus.	☐
		B	They will walk.	☐
		C	They will go on the underground.	☐
13	The total number of questions in the quiz will be	**A**	five.	☐
		B	fifteen.	☐
		C	twenty-five.	☐

14 Tony's favourite area of science is

    A biology. ☐

    B chemistry. ☐

    C physics. ☐

15 Winners of the competition get

    A T-shirts. ☐

    B cinema tickets. ☐

    C a box of chocolates. ☐

PART 4

QUESTIONS 16–20

You will hear a girl asking for information about a summer job.

Listen and complete questions 16–20.

You will hear the conversation twice.

Summer holiday job

Type of job:	Farm worker
Time working day ends:	**16** ....
You need to be:	**17** .... and careful
You will earn:	**18** £ .... a week
What you must pay for:	**19** ....
Date work begins:	**20** .... May

PART 5

QUESTIONS 21–25

You will hear the manager of a cycling club giving some information about a bike race.
Listen and complete questions 21–25.
You will hear the information twice.

Cardiff Bike Race

Date of race:		22nd September
Team colour:	**21**	
Number of people per team:	**22**	
Time of race:	**23**	.... a.m.
Food at snack place:	**24**	.... and drink
First prize:	**25**	a new ....

You now have 8 minutes to write your answers on the answer sheet.

PAPER 3 SPEAKING (8–10 minutes)

The Speaking test lasts 8 to 10 minutes. You will take the test with another candidate. There are two examiners, but only one of them will talk to you. The examiner will ask you questions and ask you to talk to the other candidate.

Part 1 (5–6 minutes)

The examiner will ask you and your partner some questions. These questions will be about your daily life, past experience and future plans. For example, you may have to speak about your school, job, hobbies or home town.

Part 2 (3–4 minutes)

You and your partner will speak to each other. You will ask and answer questions. The examiner will give you a card with some information on it. The examiner will give your partner a card with some words on it. Your partner will use the words on the card to ask you questions about the information you have. Then you will change roles.

Visual materials for Paper 3

1A

City Sports

14 High Street
Sale starts Monday 3 January
Cheap skis, snowboards and jackets
Open Monday to Saturday   9 a.m. – 6 p.m.
For more information call 846730

2B

Café

- **name / café?**

- **where?**

- **what? / sell?**

- **open / Sundays?**

- **sit outside?**

3A

Car Museum

26 Station Road
Lots of cars from famous films!
Open daily 10 a.m. – 5 p.m.
Ticket prices: Adults £7.00
                           Children £4.00
Lovely café for hot and cold snacks

4B

College Library

- **where / library?**

- **open / evenings?**

- **good computers?**

- **how / join?**

- **DVDs?**

1B

Sports Shop

- **address?**

- **what / sell?**

- **phone number?**

- **open / Friday?**

- **close?**

2A

River Island Café

Opposite the cinema

Monday – Saturday   9 a.m. – 11 p.m.

Excellent coffee and cakes

Sit inside, or in our beautiful garden

Great place to meet friends

3B

MUSEUM

- address?

- what / see?

- adult ticket? / £?

- open / Wednesdays?

- buy / food?

4A

College Library

First floor, next to art room
Open 8 a.m till 10 p.m.
Books on all subjects
DVDs to rent
24 excellent new computers
Bring student card to join library

1C

SKIING HOLIDAY

In the beautiful Blue Mountains
18–24 February
Only £800! Skis and boots included!
Stay in comfortable hotel with good views
Interested? Go to www.holiday.com

2D

Cake-making course

- date / course?

- cost? / £?

- start?

- learn / cook biscuits?

- telephone number?

3C

The Boat Show

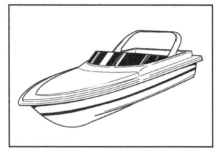

At West Park
On Sunday 5 August
Doors open 8 a.m.

Find out about all the latest boats and sailing
Buy boats, sailing clothes and shoes
www.boats.com

4D

Story-writing competition

- **competition for 16-year-olds?**

- **how many words?**

- **what / write about?**

- **email address?**

- **what / first prize?**

1D

SKIING HOLIDAY

- where / holiday?

- cost / £?

- when?

- pay extra / skis and boots?

- website?

2C

Cake-making course

<u>Saturday 6 July</u> 9 a.m. – 5 p.m.

Top chef Frank Martin will teach you to make cakes and biscuits

£50

Lunch in Frank's café
Call Frank on 866354

3D

Boat Show

- **where / show?**
- **when / show?**
- **start?**

- **what / sell?**
- **website?**

4C

Story-writing competition

For ages 15–18
Stories must be about nature
Write 500–1000 words

Best story wins a laptop!
Send stories to: david@college.com
by 5 April

Paper 3 frames

Test 1

Note: The visual materials for Paper 3 appear on pages 96–103.

Part 1 (5–6 minutes)

Greetings and introductions

At the beginning of Part 1, the interlocutor greets the candidates, asks for their names and asks them to spell something.

Giving information about place of origin, occupation, studies

The interlocutor asks the candidates about where they come from / live, and for information about their school / studies / work.

Giving general information about self

The interlocutor asks the candidates questions about their daily life, past experience or future plans. They may be asked, for example, about their likes and dislikes or about recent past experiences, or to describe and compare places.

Extended response

In the final section of Part 1, candidates are expected to give an extended response to a 'Tell me something about …' prompt. The topics are still of a personal and concrete nature. Candidates should produce at least three utterances in their extended response.

Part 2 (3–4 minutes)

The interlocutor introduces the activity as follows:

Interlocutor: *(Pablo)*, here is some information about a **sports shop**.

(Interlocutor shows answer card 1A on page 96 to Pablo)

(Laura), you don't know anything about the **sports shop**, so ask *(Pablo)* some questions about it.

(Interlocutor shows questions card 1B on page 98 to Laura)

Use these words to help you. *(Interlocutor indicates prompt words)*

Do you understand?

Now *(Laura)*, ask *(Pablo)* your questions about the **sports shop** and *(Pablo)*, you answer them.

1A

City Sports

14 High Street
Sale starts Monday 3 January
Cheap skis, snowboards and jackets
Open Monday to Saturday   9 a.m. – 6 p.m.
For more information call 846730

1B

Sports Shop

- **address?**

- **what / sell?**

- **phone number?**

- **open / Friday?**

- **close?**

When the candidates have asked and answered questions about the shop, they exchange roles and talk about a different topic.

Paper 3 frames

The interlocutor introduces the activity as follows:

Interlocutor: *(Laura)*, here is some information about a **skiing holiday**.

(Interlocutor shows answer card 1C on page 100 to Laura)

(Pablo), you don't know anything about the **skiing holiday**, so ask *(Laura)* some questions about it.

(Interlocutor shows questions card 1D on page 102 to Pablo)

Use these words to help you. *(Interlocutor indicates prompt words)*

Do you understand?

Now *(Pablo)*, ask *(Laura)* your questions about the **skiing holiday** and *(Laura)*, you answer them.

1C

SKIING HOLIDAY

In the beautiful Blue Mountains
18–24 February
Only £800! Skis and boots included!
Stay in comfortable hotel with good views
Interested? Go to www.holiday.com

1D

SKIING HOLIDAY

- **where / holiday?**
- **cost / £?**
- **when?**
- **pay extra / skis and boots?**
- **website?**

Note: Candidates are assessed on both their questions and answers in Part 2 of the test.

Test 2

Note: The visual materials for Paper 3 appear on pages 96–103.

Part 1 (5–6 minutes)

Greetings and introductions

At the beginning of Part 1, the interlocutor greets the candidates, asks for their names and asks them to spell something.

Giving information about place of origin, occupation, studies

The interlocutor asks the candidates about where they come from / live, and for information about their school / studies / work.

Giving general information about self

The interlocutor asks the candidates questions about their daily life, past experience or future plans. They may be asked, for example, about their likes and dislikes or about recent past experiences, or to describe and compare places.

Extended response

In the final section of Part 1, candidates are expected to give an extended response to a 'Tell me something about …' prompt. The topics are still of a personal and concrete nature. Candidates should produce at least three utterances in their extended response.

Part 2 (3–4 minutes)

The interlocutor introduces the activity as follows:

Interlocutor: *(Pablo)*, here is some information about a **café**.

(Interlocutor shows answer card 2A on page 98 to Pablo)

(Laura), you don't know anything about the **café**, so ask *(Pablo)* some questions about it.

(Interlocutor shows questions card 2B on page 96 to Laura)

Use these words to help you. *(Interlocutor indicates prompt words)*

Do you understand?

Now *(Laura)*, ask *(Pablo)* your questions about the **café** and *(Pablo)*, you answer them.

2A

River Island Café

Opposite the cinema
Monday – Saturday   9 a.m. – 11 p.m.
Excellent coffee and cakes
Sit inside, or in our beautiful garden
Great place to meet friends

2B

Café

- **name / café?**

- **where?**

- **what? / sell?**

- **open / Sundays?**

- **sit outside?**

When the candidates have asked and answered questions about the café, they exchange roles and talk about a different topic.

The interlocutor introduces the activity as follows:

Interlocutor: *(Laura)*, here is some information about a **cake-making course**.

    (Interlocutor shows answer card 2C on page 102 to Laura)

    (Pablo), you don't know anything about the **cake-making course**, so ask *(Laura)* some questions about it.

    (Interlocutor shows questions card 2D on page 100 to Pablo)

    Use these words to help you. *(Interlocutor indicates prompt words)*

    Do you understand?

    Now *(Pablo)*, ask *(Laura)* your questions about the **cake-making course** and *(Laura)*, you answer them.

2C

Cake-making course

<u>Saturday 6 July</u> 9 a.m. – 5 p.m.

Top chef Frank Martin will teach you to
make cakes and biscuits

£50

Lunch in Frank's café

Call Frank on 866354

2D

<u>Cake-making course</u>

- **date / course?**
- **cost? / £?**
- **start?**
- **learn / cook biscuits?**
- **telephone number?**

Note: Candidates are assessed on both their questions and answers in Part 2 of the test.

Test 3

Note: The visual materials for Paper 3 appear on pages 96–103.

Part 1 (5–6 minutes)

Greetings and introductions

At the beginning of Part 1, the interlocutor greets the candidates, asks for their names and asks them to spell something.

Giving information about place of origin, occupation, studies

The interlocutor asks the candidates about where they come from / live, and for information about their school / studies / work.

Giving general information about self

The interlocutor asks the candidates questions about their daily life, past experience or future plans. They may be asked, for example, about their likes and dislikes or about recent past experiences, or to describe and compare places.

Extended response

In the final section of Part 1, candidates are expected to give an extended response to a 'Tell me something about …' prompt. The topics are still of a personal and concrete nature. Candidates should produce at least three utterances in their extended response.

Part 2 (3–4 minutes)

The interlocutor introduces the activity as follows:

Interlocutor: *(Pablo)*, here is some information about a **car museum**.

                (Interlocutor shows answer card 3A on page 97 to Pablo)

                (Laura), you don't know anything about the **museum**, so ask *(Pablo)* some questions about it.

                (Interlocutor shows questions card 3B on page 99 to Laura)

                Use these words to help you. *(Interlocutor indicates prompt words)*

                Do you understand?

                Now *(Laura)*, ask *(Pablo)* your questions about the **museum** and *(Pablo)*, you answer them.

3A

Car Museum

26 Station Road
Lots of cars from famous films!
Open daily 10 a.m. – 5 p.m.
Ticket prices: Adults £7.00
                       Children £4.00
Lovely café for hot and cold snacks

3B

MUSEUM

- **address?**

- **what / see?**

- **adult ticket? / £?**

- **open / Wednesdays?**

- **buy / food?**

When the candidates have asked and answered questions about the museum, they exchange roles and talk about a different topic.

The interlocutor introduces the activity as follows:

Interlocutor: *(Laura)*, here is some information about a **boat show**.

(Interlocutor shows answer card 3C on page 101 to Laura)

(Pablo), you don't know anything about the **boat show**, so ask *(Laura)* some questions about it.

(Interlocutor shows questions card 3D on page 103 to Pablo)

Use these words to help you. *(Interlocutor indicates prompt words)*

Do you understand?

Now *(Pablo)*, ask *(Laura)* your questions about the **boat show** and *(Laura)*, you answer them.

3C

The Boat Show

At West Park
On Sunday 5 August
Doors open 8 a.m.

Find out about all the latest boats and sailing
Buy boats, sailing clothes, and shoes
www.boats.com

3D

Boat Show

- **where / show?**
- **when / show?**
- **start?**

- **what / sell?**
- **website?**

Note: Candidates are assessed on both their questions and answers in Part 2 of the test.

Test 4

Note: The visual materials for Paper 3 appear on pages 96–103.

Part 1 (5–6 minutes)

Greetings and introductions

At the beginning of Part 1, the interlocutor greets the candidates, asks for their names and asks them to spell something.

Giving information about place of origin, occupation, studies

The interlocutor asks the candidates about where they come from / live, and for information about their school / studies / work.

Giving general information about self

The interlocutor asks the candidates questions about their daily life, past experience or future plans. They may be asked, for example, about their likes and dislikes or about recent past experiences, or to describe and compare places.

Extended response

In the final section of Part 1, candidates are expected to give an extended response to a 'Tell me something about …' prompt. The topics are still of a personal and concrete nature. Candidates should produce at least three utterances in their extended response.

Part 2 (3–4 minutes)

The interlocutor introduces the activity as follows:

Interlocutor: *(Pablo)*, here is some information about a **college library**.

                (Interlocutor shows answer card 4A on page 99 to Pablo)

                (Laura), you don't know anything about the **college library**, so ask *(Pablo)* some questions about it.

                (Interlocutor shows questions card 4B on page 97 to Laura)

                Use these words to help you. (Interlocutor indicates prompt words)

                Do you understand?

                Now *(Laura)*, ask *(Pablo)* your questions about the **college library** and *(Pablo)*, you answer them.

4A	4B
College Library First floor, next to art room Open 8 a.m till 10 p.m. Books on all subjects DVDs to rent 24 excellent new computers Bring student card to join library	<u>**College Library**</u> • **where / library?** • **open / evenings?** • **good computers?** • **how / join?** • **DVDs?**

When the candidates have asked and answered questions about the college library, they exchange roles and talk about a different topic.

The interlocutor introduces the activity as follows:

Interlocutor: *(Laura)*, here is some information about a **story-writing competition**.

(Interlocutor shows answer card 4C on page 103 to Laura)

(Pablo), you don't know anything about the **story-writing competition**, so ask *(Laura)* some questions about it.

(Interlocutor shows questions card 4D on page 101 to Pablo)

Use these words to help you. *(Interlocutor indicates prompt words)*

Do you understand?

Now *(Pablo)*, ask *(Laura)* your questions about the **story-writing competition** and *(Laura)*, you answer them.

4C

Story-writing competition

For ages 15–18
Stories must be about nature
Write 500–1000 words

Best story wins a laptop!
Send stories to: david@college.com
by 5 April

4D

Story-writing competition

- **competition for 16-year-olds?**

- **how many words?**

- **what / write about?**

- **email address?**

- **what / first prize?**

Note: Candidates are assessed on both their questions and answers in Part 2 of the test.

Test 1 Answer Key

Paper 1   Reading and Writing

Part 1

1 H   2 C   3 G   4 B   5 F

Part 2

6 A   7 C   8 B   9 C   10 C

Part 3

11 C   12 A   13 C   14 A   15 C   16 G   17 A   18 C
19 H   20 E

Part 4

21 A   22 B   23 B   24 C   25 A   26 C   27 B

Part 5

28 A   29 C   30 A   31 B   32 B   33 C   34 A   35 C

Part 6

36 beach   37 camping   38 picnic   39 park   40 tennis

Part 7

41 by   42 it   43 much   44 when / while   45 next / this   46 than
47 would / 'd   48 for   49 what   50 hope

Part 8

51 Hip-Hop   52 Saturday   53 10 a.m. / ten o'clock   54 car
55 £7 / seven pounds

Part 9

Question 56

The three parts that must be communicated are:

i   where you last saw the bag
ii   what the bag looks like
iii what was in the bag

Sample answer A

Mark: 5

> Yeah, it is true. I lost it. I saw it yesterday at school. So, it is red and black with funny pictures. It was empty. If you see it, please tell me.

All 3 parts of the message are clearly communicated.

Sample answer B

Mark: 4

> Yes I have lost my school bag yesterday. I last saw it in the Bus. It's dark Blue coloured with white strapes on it. There's my school things and my phone. Please fing it.

All three parts of the message are communicated but there are some non-impeding errors in spelling and grammar.

Sample answer C

Mark: 3

> Hi Jem
> "Are you ok" I hope Ok. I realy lost my school bag. I don't know where I can lost it, may be in school. I remember that standard books and pens were in it.
> I come to you today.
> Danil.

Two parts of the message are clearly communicated but one part is unattempted. Only minor spelling errors or occasional grammatical errors.

Sample answer D

Mark: 2

> Hello,
> I saw at 11th of February on my table. It was black bag with word from steel "ARMANY". I went to the blackboard and when I got back it escaped.
> Goodbye.

Two parts are communicated but there are errors in expression which impede communication.

Sample answer E

Mark: 1

> I lost my Bag. Last week. It is big and yellow. Please if you find it call
> 56893569. I pleasd you find it.
> Vlad

Only one part of the message is communicated, although the candidate has made some attempt to address the task.

Sample answer F

Mark: 0

> From: Salma
> To: Aina
>
> Hallo how are you? Do you like you new school?
> Do you like you teacher, and you's news friends? My i'm very happy, of my school.
> By your friend Salma.

The content is irrelevant to the task.

Paper 2   Listening

Part 1

1 A   **2** C   **3** A   **4** B   **5** C

Part 2

6 A   **7** E   **8** G   **9** D   **10** B

Part 3

11 B   **12** A   **13** A   **14** B   **15** C

Part 4

16 45 / forty-five   **17** (£) 22 / twenty-two   **18** tea   **19** Highclere   **20** tree

Part 5

21 Friday   **22** 3.15 / a quarter past three   **23** 6 / six   **24** snacks   **25** 5 (th) July

Transcript

This is the Cambridge English: Key, Test One. There are five parts to the test. Parts One, Two, Three, Four and Five. We will now stop for a moment before we start the test. Please ask any questions now because you must NOT speak during the test.

[pause]

PART 1   *Now, look at the instructions for Part One.*

[pause]

You will hear five short conversations. You will hear each conversation twice. There is one question for each conversation. For questions 1 to 5, put a tick under the right answer.
Here is an example:
How many people were at the meeting?

Woman:	Were there many people at the meeting?
Man:	About thirty.
Woman:	That's not many.
Man:	No, but more than last time.

[pause]

The answer is C.

Now we are ready to start. Look at question one.

[pause]

Question 1   *One. Which T-shirt does the woman buy?*

Woman:	Excuse me, have you got any T-shirts for around £10?
Man:	We've got this one with a flower on for £8 and some with stars on for £7.
Woman:	I'll take the first one you showed me.
Man:	OK, I'll put that in a bag for you.

[pause]

Now listen again.

[repeat]

[pause]

Question 2   *Two. When is the girl's swimming lesson next week?*

Girl:	What time are the swimming lessons next week? Are they at 10 o'clock as usual?
Man:	Sorry, there's a swimming competition from 9 o'clock and it won't finish until 11.
Girl:	Will my lesson start after that?
Man:	Of course, all lessons will start as soon as the competition finishes.

[pause]

Now listen again.

[repeat]

[pause]

Question 3   *Three. Which bus stop does the woman need?*

Woman: Excuse me, I want to catch a bus to go to the hospital. Which bus do I need? Is it the one in front of the supermarket?

Man: Buses go to the sports centre from there. The one you want is by the train station on West Street.

Woman: Oh, thank you very much.

Man: You're welcome.

[pause]

Now listen again.

[repeat]

[pause]

Question 4   *Four. Which is the man's raincoat?*

Man: Excuse me, I left my raincoat on the bus. Did anyone find it?

Woman: Let me see. We have a few raincoats. I've got one here. It's long and has a belt.

Man: Oh, mine's short. I lost the belt, so it hasn't got one.

Woman: Oh yes, here it is. It's your lucky day!

[pause]

Now listen again.

[repeat]

[pause]

Question 5   *Five. Which is the office manager?*

Woman: Is that the new office manager over there?

Woman 2: Oh yes, with the short hair. When I last saw her, her hair was long.

Woman: And didn't she wear glasses as well?

Woman 2: Yes she did. She looks quite different now doesn't she?

[pause]

Now listen again.

[repeat]

[pause]

That is the end of Part One.

[pause]

PART 2   *Now look at Part Two.*

[pause]

Listen to Amy and James talking about planning a birthday party. What job is each person going to do? For questions 6 to 10, write a letter A to H next to each person. You will hear the conversation twice.

[pause]

Amy:	Are we nearly ready for Sally's party, James? Chris is making the cake, of course.
James:	I know, it's going to be amazing! What are you doing Amy?
Amy:	I've found a nice room above a restaurant and I'm booking it tomorrow. There's space for fifty guests so we'll be fine. And what about you, James? Are you getting the present?
James:	I'm no good at choosing presents, Amy! I'm going to call all Sally's friends and ask them to come to the party. Oh, and I spoke to Claire yesterday.
Amy:	What's she doing? If she's free, she can put up some balloons.
James:	She's thinking about the music, actually. I know Tom usually plans the music, but this time he's bringing juice and lemonade. There was a big discount at the supermarket so he got lots.
Amy:	Excellent! So, that just leaves Jane.
James:	She's getting a pair of earrings we can all give Sally for her birthday.
Amy:	That's a great idea. It's going to be an amazing party!

[pause]

Now listen again.

[repeat]

[pause]

That is the end of Part Two.

[pause]

PART 3   *Now look at Part Three.*

[pause]

Listen to Jessica talking to Frank about a dance class. For questions 11 to 15, tick A, B or C. You will hear the conversation twice. Look at questions 11 to 15 now. You have twenty seconds.

[pause]

Now listen to the conversation.

Jessica:	Hi Frank. Are you coming to the dance class at eight o'clock this evening?
Frank:	Hi Jessica. Yes, I finish work at half past seven, but I need to be home by nine. How long is the class?
Jessica:	Oh don't worry. The class is forty-five minutes long, not an hour. Some people stay later to do half an hour extra exercise, but you don't have to.
Frank:	OK. What do I need to bring?
Jessica:	Just wear comfortable sports clothes. You can leave your trainers at home, because the teacher doesn't want us to wear shoes. And bring lots to drink.
Frank:	I'm not very fit. Is that a problem?
Jessica:	No, there are people of all ages there and lots of them aren't very fit. But tell the teacher if you have never done dance classes before.
Frank:	Are the classes expensive?

Jessica: The price has just changed from five pounds to six pounds. It's still a good price, though, because other classes at the sports centre cost eight pounds.

Frank: OK, shall I come to your house at half past seven?

Jessica: I'm going straight from college. There's a café in the sports centre so let's meet there.

Frank: OK, see you later.

[pause]

Now listen again.

[repeat]

[pause]

That is the end of Part Three.

[pause]

PART 4   *Now look at Part Four.*

[pause]

You will hear a woman asking about a tour of a castle. Listen and complete questions 16 to 20. You will hear the conversation twice.

[pause]

Woman: Excuse me, can you tell me about the tours of the castle, please?

Man: Yes, of course. We have three tours a day – at ten a.m., one p.m. and three p.m.

Woman: Thanks. How long does the tour take?

Man: The normal time is forty-five minutes but we ask you to arrive fifteen minutes early so we can check how many people there are. We can't take more than twenty.

Woman: OK, that's great. Do you do a family ticket?

Man: We do, it's twenty-two pounds. Or we have an adult ticket for eight pounds and it's five pounds for children.

Woman: Where do I wait for the tour?

Man: You can wait in the café. Show them your ticket and you'll get a free tea or soft drink.

Woman: Oh, that's good. Can I visit other places after the tour?

Man: Yes, you can visit the beautiful Highclere Gardens.

Woman: Sorry, what was the name?

Man: Highclere. That's H-I-G-H-C-L-E-R-E.

Woman: Thanks, I've got that.

Man: In the garden you can see a six-hundred-year-old bridge and a really famous tree, which is eight hundred years old. Make sure you don't miss that!

Woman: Thank you very much.

[pause]

Now listen again.

[repeat]

[pause]

That is the end of Part Four.

[pause]

PART 5   *Now look at Part Five.*

[pause]

You will hear some information on the radio about a new cooking programme. Listen and complete questions 21 to 25. You will hear the information twice.

[pause]

Woman: How do you feel when you have to cook something for friends or family? Do you feel worried or even afraid? If you do, then our new cooking programme – *Cooking for Beginners* – is just for you! Every week, a famous chef will teach you how to make a different dish. The programme is on every Friday, so you can invite your friends over on Saturday to try your new dish. Before the programme, we will put a list of everything you need on our website so you can go shopping and be ready to watch from three fifteen until four thirty. Don't worry if you're not a good cook – our chefs will explain things slowly and clearly. There will be six programmes in total and you will learn how to make more than twenty dishes, including snacks, main courses and cakes. So, we hope to find you waiting in your kitchen for the first programme on the fifth of July, when Chris White will teach you how to make your first dish. Happy cooking!

[pause]

Now listen again.

[repeat]

[pause]

That is the end of Part Five.

You now have eight minutes to write your answers on the answer sheet.

Note: Teacher, stop the recording here and time eight minutes. Remind students when there is **one** minute remaining.

[pause]

That is the end of the test.

Test 2 Answer Key

PAPER 1 Reading and Writing

Part 1

1 C **2** G **3** B **4** F **5** D

Part 2

6 C **7** A **8** B **9** A **10** B

Part 3

11 A **12** B **13** C **14** C **15** B **16** D **17** E **18** G **19** B **20** A

Part 4

21 C **22** A **23** B **24** A **25** C **26** A **27** A

Part 5

28 B **29** A **30** A **31** C **32** B **33** C **34** C **35** A

Part 6

36 plane **37** station **38** passport **39** map **40** airport

Part 7

41 to **42** or **43** if / whether **44** ago **45** because / as

46 on **47** a **48** Do **49** is **50** him

Part 8

51 Rosy's Story
52 Saturday
53 8 p.m. / eight o'clock
54 3 / three tickets
55 £5 / five pounds

Part 9

Question 56

The three parts that must be communicated are:

i   your invitation to Charley to come to your picnic
ii where Charley should meet you
iii what Charley should bring with him / her

Sample answer A

Mark: 5

> Hi Charley
> How are you? I'm going to ask you one thing, can you come to La Antilla next Saturday? Because I'm planning a picnic. And if you can come, can you bring sweets and potatoes chips?
> See you
> Maria

All three parts of the message are very clearly communicated.

Sample answer B

Mark: 4

> Hello Charley I am your friend Anais I want to tell you that the next Saturday I am going to do a picnic. We are going to meet in the center park. You have to bring some drinks.
> Good bay.

All three parts of the message are communicated but there are some non-impeding errors and awkwardness of expression.

Sample answer C

Mark: 3

> Hello Charley
> Do you come in my picnic? Is my birthday!! Is in forest on front in my house. Can you bring olives, potatoes...
> See you later

All three parts of the message are attempted. Expression requires interpretation by the reader.

Sample answer D

Mark: 2

> Hi Charley
> I invite you for go a forest for a picnic. In my house we play a computer game. You go on Saturday evening. Can you bring a videogame.
> See you on Saturday!

Only two parts of the message are communicated. The errors in expression may require patience and interpretation by the reader.

Sample answer E

Mark: 1

> Hi Charley
> Next Saturday I will be to make a picnic, do you want to come? If you can't come call me please.

Only one part of the message is communicated.

Sample answer F

Mark: 0

> Hello Charley
> I should to meet everything. And provably next the picnic go to playing tennis.

The response is totally incomprehensible and is under length.

Paper 2   Listening

Part 1

1 C   **2** B   **3** C   **4** A   **5** A

Part 2

6 B   **7** H   **8** E   **9** D   **10** G

Part 3

11 C   **12** B   **13** B   **14** A   **15** B

Part 4

16 825 / eight hundred and twenty-five   **17** 15 / fifteen   **18** 2 / two
19 sofa   **20** Monday

Part 5

21 (£) 79 / seventy-nine   **22** 3 (p.m. / o'clock)
23 Myatt   **24** 99365412704   **25** photo

Transcript

This is the Cambridge English: Key, Test Two. There are five parts to the test. Parts One, Two, Three, Four and Five. We will now stop for a moment before we start the test. Please ask any questions now because you must NOT speak during the test.

[pause]

PART 1   *Now, look at the instructions for Part One.*

[pause]

You will hear five short conversations. You will hear each conversation twice. There is one question for each conversation. For questions 1 to 5, put a tick under the right answer.
Here is an example:
How many people were at the meeting?

Woman: Were there many people at the meeting?

Man: About thirty.

Woman: That's not many.

Man: No, but more than last time.

[pause]

The answer is C.
Now we are ready to start. Look at question one.

[pause]

Question 1   *One. What does the woman order?*

Man: Are you ready to order?

Woman: The burger looks good. Does it come with anything?

Man: You can have it with salad or chips. If you'd like both, it's a bit extra.

Woman: I'll do that. I don't mind paying a bit more.

[pause]

Now listen again.

[repeat]

[pause]

Question 2   *Two. What size boots is the woman going to try on next?*

Woman: Do you have these boots in a bigger size? I've tried them in a thirty-seven, but they're too small.

Man: Do you want to try them in a thirty-eight or a thirty-nine? I can get them for you.

Woman: I think the thirty-nine will be too big.

Man: OK. I'll be back in a moment.

Now listen again.

[repeat]

[pause]

Question 3   *Three. Where will the man get off the bus?*

Man: I'm going to the college. Where should I get off the bus?

Woman: There's a stop by the supermarket and another next to the park. They're both near the college.

Man: I've got plenty of time, so the stop by the park is best. I can go for a walk first before I go to the college.

Woman: OK, I'll tell you when we get there.

[pause]

Now listen again.

[repeat]

[pause]

Question 4   *Four. How many books does the boy want to borrow now?*

Boy: Can I borrow these three books, please?

Woman: Let me see. You have already borrowed six books and you can't borrow more than eight.

Boy: That's OK. I have two books to return as well.

Woman: OK, please return those books first before you borrow any more.

[pause]

Now listen again.

[repeat]

[pause]

Question 5   *Five. What job does Mark's brother do?*

Woman: Mark, does your brother still work at that expensive hotel?

Mark: He's still there but he's not a receptionist any more.

Woman: Really? Why not? He was really good at it!

Mark: I know! He's a waiter at the moment, and he hopes to be a chef one day, because he really loves cooking.

[pause]

Now listen again.

[repeat]

[pause]

That is the end of Part One.

[pause]

PART 2   *Now look at Part Two.*

[pause]

Listen to Emily and John talking about activities they did last weekend. Which activity did each person do? For questions 6 to 10, write a letter A to H next to each person. You will hear the conversation twice.

[pause]

Emily:	Did you have a good weekend, John? I heard you went on a sailing trip.
John:	It was too expensive, so I just went fishing. I saw Pete on his bike a lot. He went all the way to the beach! What did you do, Emily?
Emily:	I played tennis with my brother. I wanted to play basketball, but I couldn't find anyone to play with.
John:	Why didn't you ask Jenny? Oh no, that's right, she was busy at the park. There was a skateboarding competition.
Emily:	I hope she won a prize. Did you hear about Joe? He broke his leg playing football!
John:	Oh no, that will stop him going swimming with me next weekend!
Emily:	Are you going to the beach? I'll come with you – I love it there.
John:	OK, we can ask Andy as well. He played a lot of table-tennis this weekend, but he says he wants to do something outside next weekend.
Emily:	Great, I'll ask him if he wants to come. We can go to East Beach.

[pause]

Now listen again.

[repeat]

[pause]

That is the end of Part Two.

[pause]

PART 3   *Now look at Part Three.*

[pause]

Listen to Suzy talking to a friend about a new shop. For questions 11 to 15, tick A, B or C. You will hear the conversation twice. Look at questions 11 to 15 now. You have twenty seconds.

[pause]

Now listen to the conversation.

Suzy:	A new clothes shop opened in the town last week. I went there yesterday and I'm going back again today!
Woman:	Do you mean the one near your college, Suzy?
Suzy:	That's been there a long time, in fact they're opening another one in the shopping centre. The one I'm talking about is across the road from the newsagent's.
Woman:	What does it sell?
Suzy:	It sells shoes and boots as well as clothes. The only thing missing is bags!
Woman:	What time does it open?

Suzy:	It's normally open from ten 'til six, but it stays open until eight p.m. on a Thursday.
Woman:	So, is it open every day of the week? I'd like to go on Tuesday.
Suzy:	That's fine. The only day it's closed at the moment is Monday, but it will open every day if it's popular enough.
Woman:	Oh, OK. I'm looking for some work. Do they need any staff?
Suzy:	Yes, they need shop assistants. The sign in the window says, if you are interested, go in and talk to the manager. Don't phone, because they're very busy.
Woman:	Oh great, I'll just write that down. Thanks, Suzy.

[pause]

Now listen again.

[repeat]

[pause]

That is the end of Part Three.

[pause]

PART 4 *Now look at Part Four.*

[pause]

You will hear a man phoning about a flat he wants to rent. Listen and complete questions 16 to 20. You will hear the conversation twice.

[pause]

Man:	Hello. I'm calling about the flat that you have to rent on Green Street.
Woman:	Oh yes. Twenty-five A, Green Street? It's a lovely flat.
Man:	How much is it?
Woman:	Well, it was eight hundred and seventy-five pounds a month, but the price has gone down, so now it's only eight hundred and twenty-five pounds. That's a great price.
Man:	Is it far from the station?
Woman:	You can walk there in fifteen minutes or there's a bus which takes just five minutes.
Man:	Great. How many bedrooms does it have?
Woman:	There are five rooms in total – two bedrooms, a living room, a bathroom and a kitchen.
Man:	It's quite big! Does it have any furniture?
Woman:	There's a really nice table and a sofa, but there are no beds.
Man:	That's not a problem. The flat sounds perfect. Can I go and see it?
Woman:	There are people living there at the moment, but they're leaving on Friday.
Man:	OK. I can meet you there on Saturday.
Woman:	Monday's better for me.
Man:	Perfect. See you then.

[pause]

Now listen again.

[repeat]

[pause]

That is the end of Part Four.

[pause]

PART 5   *Now look at Part Five.*

[pause]

You will hear some information for new students about a college. Listen and complete questions 21 to 25. You will hear the information twice.

[pause]

Man: I'd like to welcome you all to Langley College. I hope you have a great time studying here. Our first classes are next Wednesday, but today you have a chance to visit the college. We're very lucky to have a modern sports centre for you to use. It's not expensive. You only pay seventy-nine pounds to become a member of the sports centre for twelve months, or you can pay six pounds seventy each time you go. We also have a café which is open on weekdays from ten a.m. to three p.m. You'll meet your teachers at four p.m. today to get more information about your course but if you have any questions about the college, you can speak to the receptionist, Mrs Myatt – that's M-Y-A-double T. She is here from Monday to Friday but if you can't come in, you can call her on double nine-three-six-five-four-one-two-seven-o-four. When you come back on Wednesday, you'll need to give us a photo. We need that for your student ID card. Those will be ready for you to collect next Friday.

[pause]

Now listen again.

[repeat]

[pause]

That is the end of Part Five.

You now have eight minutes to write your answers on the answer sheet.

Note: Teacher, stop the recording here and time eight minutes. Remind students when there is **one** minute remaining.

[pause]

That is the end of the test.

Test 3 Answer Key

PAPER 1   Reading and Writing

Part 1

1 G   **2** E   **3** H   **4** D   **5** A

Part 2

6 B   **7** C   **8** B   **9** A   **10** A

Part 3

11 C   **12** C   **13** C   **14** B   **15** A   **16** E   **17** H   **18** G   **19** C   **20** A

Part 4

21 B   **22** A   **23** B   **24** A   **25** C   **26** B   **27** B

Part 5

28 B   **29** A   **30** C   **31** A   **32** C   **33** A   **34** B   **35** C

Part 6

36 wallet   **37** bank   **38** chemist   **39** café   **40** bus

Part 7

41 what / how   **42** have   **43** of   **44** if   **45** a   **46** am / 'm   **47** why
48 Can / Could   **49** by   **50** from / with

Part 8

51 4 p.m. / four o'clock
52 £85 / eighty-five pounds
53 Thursday
54 Julie
55 2 / two

Part 9

Question 56

The three parts that must be communicated are:

i   where the concert is
ii   what time the concert starts
iii   details of how you're going to get to the concert

Sample answer A

Mark: 5

> Hi, Sami!
> The concert is in the front of Palas Jasi. It's start at 6pm, but we cam
> be there at 5pm because will be crowded. We will get there by a taxi.
> Your friend, Rares

All three parts of the message are clearly communicated with occasional spelling or grammatical errors.

Sample answer B

Mark: 4

> Hey Sami! The concert is at the new scene at Short street, at 7 P.M.
> until 11PM I think. I'm going to get there with a cab. Meet me at home at
> 6.30 P.M. See you there. Bye

There are some non-impeding errors in grammar but all three parts of the message are clearly communicated.

Sample answer C

Mark: 3

> Hi Sami! The concert was very well It was near the high street. It start at
> 6pm. Take the bus on station number eight and go three station.

All three parts of the message are included but the context is incorrect as the concert is in the future not the past.

Sample answer D

Mark: 2

> Dear Samy,
> How you sad, next Friday is the concert, it start nine o'clock in the
> Yulius mall.
> I am going in the Yulius mall whit my friend, Maddlima.
> See you in Yulius mall! By!

Only two parts of the message are communicated and the response requires patience and interpretation by the reader.

Sample answer E

Mark: 1

> Hello Sami!
> I want to tell you about the consert vich will was next Friday. His name is AC/DC. Consert started at 19.00 and fineshed at 21.00. This consert was about Georges dance.
> See you Sami!

Some attempt is made to address the task but the response is very unclear.

Sample answer F

Mark: 0

> Hello, Sami how do you do? You come to school? I did is very good friends you. 'Goodbye Sami'

The response is incomprehensible.

Paper 2   Listening

Part 1

1 A   **2** C   **3** A   **4** A   **5** B

Part 2

6 A   **7** F   **8** B   **9** C   **10** E

Part 3

11 C   **12** A   **13** A   **14** C   **15** B

Part 4

16 pink   **17** Spring   **18** September   **19** 40 / forty   **20** 8 / eight

Part 5

21 train   **22** 1.15 / a quarter past one   **23** fishing   **24** (£) 12 / twelve   **25** Aster

This is the Cambridge English: Key, Test Three. There are five parts to the test. Parts One, Two, Three, Four and Five. We will now stop for a moment before we start the test. Please ask any questions now because you must NOT speak during the test.

[pause]

PART 1   *Now, look at the instructions for Part One.*

[pause]

You will hear five short conversations. You will hear each conversation twice. There is one question for each conversation. For questions 1 to 5, put a tick under the right answer.
Here is an example:
How many people were at the meeting?

Woman: Were there many people at the meeting?

Man: About thirty.

Woman: That's not many.

Man: No, but more than last time.

[pause]

The answer is C.

Now we are ready to start. Look at question one.

[pause]

Question 1   *One. What instrument is Edward learning to play?*

Woman: Do you want to come to a piano concert with me this evening, Edward?

Edward: I'd like to, Aunt Lucy, but I can't. I've got my music lesson.

Woman: Oh, OK. I hear you're still learning the guitar. It's a pity you stopped learning the piano.

Edward: It was so hard. I really want to play the drums, but Mum thinks they're too noisy.

[pause]

Now listen again.

[repeat]

[pause]

Question 2   *Two. What will Anna have for breakfast today?*

Man: Morning, Anna. What would you like for breakfast? Some cereal and fruit?

Anna: I have that every day. Can I have an omelette today?

Man: Sorry – I've just eaten the last egg. Do you want some bread and jam instead?

Anna:	Well OK, I suppose so. Maybe I can have an omelette tomorrow.

[pause]

Now listen again.

[repeat]

[pause]

Question 3 *Three. How much is the watch?*

Man: How much is this watch? I'm looking for one that's around twenty euros.

Woman: That one's in the sale. It's eighteen euros now.

Man: Oh, what was the full price?

Woman: It was twenty-two euros until this morning.

[pause]

Now listen again.

[repeat]

[pause]

Question 4 *Four. What does Mandy's brother do?*

Man: Hello Mandy! I saw your brother at the university yesterday. He was talking to the receptionist. Is he still studying there?

Mandy: He finished studying last year and they asked him to teach some classes.

Man: That's interesting. Is he enjoying it?

Mandy: He loves it!

[pause]

Now listen again.

[repeat]

[pause]

Question 5 *Five. Who is coming to stay this weekend?*

Boy: Mum, can my friend Josh come and stay this weekend?

Woman: There won't be space, I'm sorry. Auntie Susie's coming with her baby. And you'll want to spend some time with your new cousin.

Boy: OK. You're right. What about next weekend?

Woman: That'll be fine. Grandma's coming but that's not a problem.

[pause]

Now listen again.

[repeat]

[pause]

That is the end of Part One.

[pause]

PART 2   *Now look at Part Two.*

[pause]

Listen to the conversation between Sally and her father about a computer course. How many free places are there on the computer course each day? For questions 6 to 10, write a letter A to H next to each day. You will hear the conversation twice.

[pause]

Man: Sally, let's look on the Internet and see if there are any free places for you and Emma to do that computer course one day next week.

Sally: OK, Dad. Here's the information. Let's try Monday …

Man: They've got three places then, so that's possible.

Sally: Tuesday will be better. Emma works on Mondays. Oh dear, the course is full that day.

Man: What about Wednesday? I'm free then so I can drive you there.

Sally: Let's see. It says seven places are taken and there are five left.

Man: Good. Let's ask Emma if that's OK.

Sally: Let me just check the other days first. So, Thursday …

Man: Only one left and you need two places. So that's no good. Are you busy on Friday?

Sally: Not until seven. Oh. They've only got room for two more students.

Man: You must decide quickly or it may be full. Oh look. There are courses on Saturday too, in smaller groups of six.

Sally: And there is space for four more people then. I'll see what Emma thinks.

[pause]

Now listen again.

[repeat]

[pause]

That is the end of Part Two.

[pause]

PART 3   *Now look at Part Three.*

[pause]

Listen to Stephen talking to Jenny about making some soup. For questions 11 to 15, tick A, B or C. You will hear the conversation twice. Look at questions 11 to 15 now. You have twenty seconds.

[pause]

Now listen to the conversation.

Stephen: This soup is amazing, Jenny. Do you use fresh tomatoes to make it?

Jenny: No, Stephen. I just use a can of tomatoes. Some people think roast tomatoes are best, but that's too much hard work for me.

Stephen: Who taught you how to make it?

Jenny:	My aunt's friend gave the instructions to my mother, who changed them a bit, then taught me.
Stephen:	It's not too thin, is it?
Jenny:	That's because I don't use much water. At first, I used four cups, then three, but I think two is best really.
Stephen:	So, what else is in it?
Jenny:	Some butter, an onion, the tomatoes, salt and pepper, and to make it really nice, a cup of milk. It's much cheaper than cream, you know.
Stephen:	Mmm. How long does it take to make?
Jenny:	No longer than twenty minutes. You fry the onion for five minutes, add everything else, then boil for about ten.
Stephen:	So, what are we having for the main course?
Jenny:	Well, we're having fruit cake for dessert, and for main course we've got pasta. I wanted to do lemon chicken, but I didn't have time.
Stephen:	Lovely!

[pause]

Now listen again.

[repeat]

[pause]

That is the end of Part Three.

[pause]

PART 4   *Now look at Part Four.*

[pause]

You will hear a boy asking for information about a plant. Listen and complete questions 16 to 20. You will hear the conversation twice.

[pause]

Woman:	Welcome to York Garden Centre! How can I help you?
Boy:	I'm looking for a plant for my mum's birthday. What's this one called?
Woman:	Sweet William. Some people think its name comes from the writer William Shakespeare.
Boy:	That's interesting. What colour will the flowers be on this one?
Woman:	This type is pink, but they can also be red or purple. It'll be very pretty.
Boy:	Good. When will the flowers come?
Woman:	Every spring. Then you need to cut them before the summer, so they return next year.
Boy:	OK. When should I put it outside?
Woman:	Well, it's August now. Wait until September to put it in the garden.
Boy:	How tall will it grow?
Woman:	Some types are only fifteen centimetres tall, but in two or three years this one'll be forty centimetres tall. Leave space for it!
Boy:	I'd like to buy it. How much is it?

Woman:	The normal price is ten pounds but it's only eight pounds this weekend because we have a special discount.
Boy:	Great!

[pause]

Now listen again.

[repeat]

[pause]

That is the end of Part Four.

[pause]

Now look at Part Five.

[pause]

You will hear some information about a day trip. Listen and complete questions 21 to 25. You will hear the information twice.

[pause]

Woman: Good morning students! I hope you're enjoying your stay here in the mountains. Now, I've got some information about tomorrow's day trip to North Lake. The bus is always very busy at this time of year, so we'll take the train. You'll see some beautiful countryside on the journey. To join the trip, please be here at one fifteen. You can have lunch in the café here at twelve thirty before we go. When we're there, you can choose to go walking with me, or fishing with Mr Thomas. But no swimming – the water's too cold at this time of year. Your ticket will cost eight pounds and you'll want some money to spend at the shop so bring twelve pounds, please. Now, this is important. We'll meet to return to the station at the end of the day outside the Aster Hotel, next to the lake. That's A-S-T-E-R. So, who would like to come?

[pause]

Now listen again.

[repeat]

[pause]

That is the end of Part Five.

You now have eight minutes to write your answers on the answer sheet.

[pause]

Note: Teacher, stop the recording here and time eight minutes. Remind students when there is **one** minute remaining.

That is the end of the test.

Test 4 Answer Key

PAPER 1   Reading and Writing

Part 1

1 E   **2** G   **3** A   **4** B   **5** D

Part 2

6 C   **7** B   **8** A   **9** C   **10** A

Part 3

11 C   **12** B   **13** A   **14** B   **15** B   **16** F   **17** C   **18** G   **19** B   **20** A

Part 4

21 A   **22** B   **23** A   **24** B   **25** C   **26** C   **27** B

Part 5

28 C   **29** B   **30** C   **31** A   **32** B   **33** A   **34** B   **35** A

Part 6

36 presents   **37** dress   **38** juice   **39** games   **40** card

Part 7

41 me   **42** a   **43** than   **44** no   **45** much   **46** Do   **47** to   **48** or
49 of   **50** it

Part 8

51 Better Photos
52 £12.50 / twelve pounds fifty
53 David Fox
54 786861
55 10(th) June

Part 9

Question 56

The three parts that must be communicated are:

i   what you did yesterday
ii a description of the weather
iii details of when you are coming home

Sample answer A

Mark: 5

> Hey Jo,
> Paris is wonderful.
> Yesterday I visited the eiffel tower, which is very impressive.
> The weather is lovely, it is always sunny and about 25°C.
> I will be back in 2 weeks.
> See you,
> Anna

All three parts of the message are very clearly communicated.

Sample answer B

Mark: 4

> Hello Jo,
> Yesterday I go with my father at the mountains, I climbed all day the mountain. The weather is very nice is sun and very hot. I'm coming home this afternoon.

All three parts of the message are communicated but with some non-impeding errors and some awkwardness.

Sample answer C

Mark: 3

> Hi Jo,
> Yesterday I have a nice day. I swam in the sea, went to a café.
> There's hot but sometimes it rains I think I'll come home for 3 days.
> See you later,
> Mary

All three parts of the message are communicated but there are some impeding errors and the response requires some interpretation by the reader.

Sample answer D

Mark: 2

> Hello, I'm Arthur. I'm on holiday. I'm very happy. I swim yesterday. The water
> was very good. I'm coming home in 18.02.2013.
> Arthur

Only two parts of the message are communicated. Instead of writing about the
weather, the candidate writes about water.

Sample answer E

Mark: 1

> Dear Jo,
> I hope you're fine. I'm in Spain and I have a good time. I'll be there for two
> weeks. And where will you go on your holidays? Write me soon.
> Hugs,
> Valera

Only one part of the message is communicated although there is an attempt at a
response.

Sample answer F

Mark: 0

> Paul, this is my dog Bella. It is small, she's colour is black and brown and
> she is Jorkshaier Terier. She's eyes is big and blak. Bella can stay in tow
> foot and run very speed. She is a puppy dog.

The question is unattempted in terms of not being responded to in the correct way.

PAPER 2   Listening

Part 1

1 A   **2** B   **3** B   **4** C   **5** B

Part 2

6 F   **7** D   **8** C   **9** A   **10** E

Part 3

11 C   **12** A   **13** C   **14** C   **15** B

Part 4

16 2 (p.m. / o'clock)   **17** strong   **18** (£) 300 / three hundred
19 bus ticket   **20** 24 (th)

Part 5

21 blue   **22** 3 / three   **23** 8.30 / eight-thirty
24 cake   **25** watch

Transcript

This is the Cambridge English: Key, Test Four. There are five parts to the test. Parts One, Two, Three, Four and Five. We will now stop for a moment before we start the test. Please ask any questions now because you must NOT speak during the test.

[pause]

PART 1 Now, look at the instructions for Part One.

[pause]

You will hear five short conversations. You will hear each conversation twice. There is one question for each conversation. For questions 1 to 5, put a tick under the right answer. Here is an example:
How many people were at the meeting?

Woman: Were there many people at the meeting?
Man: About thirty.
Woman: That's not many.
Man: No, but more than last time.

[pause]

The answer is C.

Now we are ready to start. Look at question one.

[pause]

Question 1 One. How will they travel to the pop concert?

Boy: I'm really excited about the pop concert tonight, Susan. Is your dad taking us by car?
Susan: He can't – he's going out.
Boy: Never mind. What about the bus? I think it stops near the stadium.
Susan: Great idea! And it'll be much cheaper than a taxi.

[pause]

Now listen again.

[repeat]

[pause]

Question 2 Two. What was the weather like on Beth's holiday?

Man: Hi Beth! How was your holiday at the beach?

Beth:	We had a great time, but it was more cloudy than it usually is in July. I prefer it when it's really sunny.
Man:	That's a shame!
Beth:	It was OK. At least it didn't rain.

[pause]

Now listen again.

[repeat]

[pause]

Question 3   *Three. Where has the teacher put the dictionaries?*

Boy:	Mrs Fletcher, I need a dictionary for this question, but there aren't any on the shelf.
Teacher:	I've moved them to the library, Peter. Students were taking them from the classroom and leaving them in the café after lunch.
Boy:	OK. Can I go and get one?
Teacher:	Yes, of course. Bring it back to the classroom.

[pause]

Now listen again

[repeat]

[pause]

Question 4   *Four. Where did Paul go running yesterday?*

Woman:	You left your trainers outside yesterday evening, Paul. They're very dirty! Did you run home through the farmer's fields?
Paul:	That way takes too long. I followed a path through the woods. It was quite wet.
Woman:	Isn't your normal way by the river?
Paul:	It is, but they closed the path to repair it. It's open again today.

[pause]

Now listen again.

[repeat]

[pause]

Question 5   *Five. What does Karen still need to get for the school play?*

Karen:	Dad, can I borrow something from you for the school play? I've got to be a film star who's running away from some photographers.
Man:	Sure, Karen. What about my black hat?
Karen:	I've got a dark hat already. But can I take your sunglasses? They'll look good together.
Man:	Fine. With your long coat, you'll have a great costume.

[pause]

Now listen again.

[repeat]

[pause]

That is the end of Part One.

[pause]

PART 2 *Now look at Part Two.*

[pause]

Listen to Gemma telling a friend about her visits to different countries. What did she like most about each country? For questions 6 to 10, write a letter A to H next to each country. You will hear the conversation twice.

[pause]

Boy: Hi Gemma. How was France?

Gemma: The hotel was a bit small but the weather was great.

Boy: You're always going away.

Gemma: Well, my dad's a journalist, so we travel a lot.

Boy: What did you like most about Italy?

Gemma: The shopping! My mum bought me a really cool swimming costume there!

Boy: Where else have you been?

Gemma: Mexico …

Boy: Wow!

Gemma: We had some amazing meals there. I enjoyed that more than being on the beach!

Boy: And you've visited India. You told us that in Geography class.

Gemma: Yes. My mum's cousin is a tennis coach – he works in a hotel there.

Boy: Is that where you stayed?

Gemma: Yes, but then we visited the countryside in the north. I loved being there. But it was a bit too hot for me.

Boy: Oh …

Gemma: I've been to Australia too! We visited a famous zoo. That was the best part of the trip. Dad had to write an article about it.

Boy: Ha ... I'd like to visit Canada.

Gemma: I've been there. The mountains are beautiful, but I loved being at our hotel most. It was wonderful.

Boy: You're so lucky!

Gemma: I know.

[pause]

Now listen again.

[repeat]

[pause]

That is the end of Part Two.

[pause]

PART 3 *Now look at Part Three.*

[pause]

Listen to Tony talking to Lisa about a science club competition. For questions 11 to 15, tick A, B or C. You will hear the conversation twice. Look at questions 11 to 15 now. You have twenty seconds.

[pause]

Now listen to the conversation.

Tony: You know my after-school science club, Lisa? There's a competition with another school, and I'm in the team!

Lisa: Well done! When is it?

Tony: The club meets on Monday, but the competition is on Wednesday. We're going to practise on Tuesday.

Lisa: Can I come and watch the competition?

Tony: Yes, but it's not at the school – it's at the university, in the building near the town hall.

Lisa: So, how will you get there?

Tony: It's too far to walk, so we'll take the bus. The underground is quicker, but it's expensive.

Lisa: I know. So, is it a quiz?

Tony: Yes. It'll take about forty-five minutes for five questions on five subjects – that's twenty-five questions. There's a fifteen minute break in the middle.

Lisa: What subjects are you hoping for?

Tony: I'm not great at biology! I enjoy physics the most. But I think this competition will have lots of questions on chemistry.

Lisa: Is there a prize?

Tony: Yes. First prize is cinema tickets for everyone in the team. Much better than a box of chocolates. And even if we don't win, we can all keep our special T-shirts.

Lisa: Cool! Good luck!

Tony: Thanks!

[pause]

Now listen again.

[repeat]

[pause]

That is the end of Part Three.

[pause]

PART 4 *Now look at Part Four.*

[pause]

You will hear a girl asking for information about a summer job. Listen and complete questions 16 to 20. You will hear the conversation twice.

[pause]

Man: Good morning. South Field Farm. How can I help?

Girl: I'm phoning about your job advertisement in this week's newspaper.

Man: Yes. We're looking for a student to be a farm worker during the holidays.

Girl: What are the hours?

Man: You'll start at six-thirty am and finish at two p.m. There's a break for lunch at twelve fifteen.

Girl: OK. Are you looking for anything special?

Man: You'll be working with soft fruit, so it's important that you're careful and strong – the boxes get heavy.

Girl:	Is the money good?
Man:	Our farm workers usually get three hundred and twenty-five pounds a week, but in this job you'll get three hundred pounds a week.
Girl:	Why's that?
Man:	Because lunch is included. But you do have to pay for your bus tickets.
Girl:	OK. I'd like the job. What should I do now?
Man:	You need to send me your details, including your address and phone number, before the tenth of May. The job starts on the twenty-fourth of May. I'll let you know next week if we need you.

[pause]

Now listen again.

[repeat]

[pause]

That is the end of Part Four.

[pause]

PART 5 *Now look at Part Five.*

[pause]

You will hear the manager of a cycling club giving some information about a bike race. Listen and complete questions 21 to 25. You will hear the information twice.

[pause]

Man: Good evening everyone, and thanks for coming to the cycling club meeting. Now, every year we enter teams in the Cardiff Bike Race, so here's some information about this year's competition. Pens ready? OK. The race is next week, on the twenty-second of September. You can't wear your normal black T-shirts and shorts because another club uses those colours. We'll wear blue instead. Make sure you pack the right ones, please. There'll be four teams with three people on each team. Steven, Petra, Luke and Alice – you've been before so you can help the others. On the day, make sure you get up and have breakfast by seven a.m., so when the race starts at eight-thirty, you're ready. At twenty kilometres, there'll be a place for snacks, with cake and orange juice. No chocolate, I'm afraid! Don't have too much or you'll feel sick. Last year's first prize was cycling shirts. This year, the winners will each get the latest sports watch! Good luck everyone!

[pause]

Now listen again.

[repeat]

[pause]

That is the end of Part Five.

You now have eight minutes to write your answers on the answer sheet.

[pause]

That is the end of the test.

Sample answer sheet – Reading and Writing (Sheet 1)

CAMBRIDGE ENGLISH
Language Assessment
Part of the University of Cambridge

Candidate Name
If not already printed, write name
in CAPITALS and complete the
Candidate No. grid (in pencil).

Candidate Signature

Examination Title

Centre

Supervisor:
If the candidate is ABSENT or has WITHDRAWN shade here ▭

Centre No.

Candidate No.

Examination
Details

0	0	0	0
1	1	1	1
2	2	2	2
3	3	3	3
4	4	4	4
5	5	5	5
6	6	6	6
7	7	7	7
8	8	8	8
9	9	9	9

KET Paper 1 Reading and Writing Candidate Answer Sheet

Instructions

Use a PENCIL (B or HB).
Rub out any answer you want to change with an eraser.

For **Parts 1, 2, 3, 4** and **5**:
Mark ONE letter for each question.
For example, if you think **C** is the right answer to the
question, mark your answer sheet like this:

0 A B C

Part 1

1 A B C D E F G H
2 A B C D E F G H
3 A B C D E F G H
4 A B C D E F G H
5 A B C D E F G H

Part 2

6 A B C
7 A B C
8 A B C
9 A B C
10 A B C

Part 3

11 A B C
12 A B C
13 A B C
14 A B C
15 A B C

16 A B C D E F G H
17 A B C D E F G H
18 A B C D E F G H
19 A B C D E F G H
20 A B C D E F G H

Part 4

21 A B C
22 A B C
23 A B C
24 A B C
25 A B C
26 A B C
27 A B C

Part 5

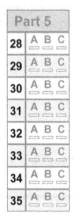

28 A B C
29 A B C
30 A B C
31 A B C
32 A B C
33 A B C
34 A B C
35 A B C

Turn over for
Parts 6 - 9 →

Sample answer sheet – Reading and Writing (Sheet 2)

For **Parts 6, 7 and 8:**

Write your answers in the spaces next to the numbers (36 to 55) like this:

0	example

Part 6		Do not write here
36		1 36 0
37		1 37 0
38		1 38 0
39		1 39 0
40		1 40 0

Part 7		Do not write here
41		1 41 0
42		1 42 0
43		1 43 0
44		1 44 0
45		1 45 0
46		1 46 0
47		1 47 0
48		1 48 0
49		1 49 0
50		1 50 0

Part 8		Do not write here
51		1 51 0
52		1 52 0
53		1 53 0
54		1 54 0
55		1 55 0

Part 9 (Question 56): Write your answer below.

Do not write below (Examiner use only).					
0	1	2	3	4	5

Sample answer sheet – Listening

Candidate Name
If not already printed, write name
in CAPITALS and complete the
Candidate No. grid (in pencil).

Candidate Signature

Examination Title

Centre

Supervisor:
If the candidate is ABSENT or has WITHDRAWN shade here ⊑⊐

Centre No.

Candidate No.

Examination Details

0	0	0	0
1	1	1	1
2	2	2	2
3	3	3	3
4	4	4	4
5	5	5	5
6	6	6	6
7	7	7	7
8	8	8	8
9	9	9	9

KET Paper 2 Listening Candidate Answer Sheet

Instructions

Use a PENCIL (B or HB).

Rub out any answer you want to change with an eraser.
For **Parts 1, 2** and **3**:
Mark ONE letter for each question.
For example, if you think **C** is the right answer to the
question, mark your answer sheet like this:

0   A B C

Part 1	Part 2	Part 3
1 A B C	6 A B C D E F G H	11 A B C
2 A B C	7 A B C D E F G H	12 A B C
3 A B C	8 A B C D E F G H	13 A B C
4 A B C	9 A B C D E F G H	14 A B C
5 A B C	10 A B C D E F G H	15 A B C

For **Parts 4** and **5**:
Write your answers in the spaces next to the
numbers (16 to 25) like this:

0   example

Part 4		Do not write here
16		1 16 0
17		1 17 0
18		1 18 0
19		1 19 0
20		1 20 0

Part 5		Do not write here
21		1 21 0
22		1 22 0
23		1 23 0
24		1 24 0
25		1 25 0